It Happened In Rhode Island

Remarkable Events That Shaped History

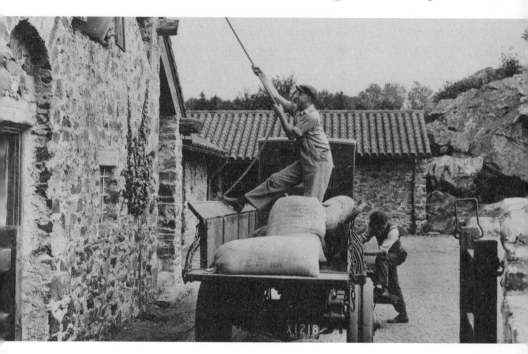

Seth Brown

Guilford, Connecticut

Copyright © 2012 by Morris Book Publishing, LLC

Map by Melissa Baker © Morris Book Publishing, LLC
Project editor: Lynn Zelem
Layout: Justin Marciano

Library of Congress Cataloging-in-Publication Data

Brown, Seth.
  It happened in Rhode Island : remarkable events that shaped history /
Seth Brown. — First edition.
       pages cm. — (It happened in series)
  Includes bibliographical references and index.
  ISBN 978-0-7627-6974-2
  1. Rhode Island—History—Anecdotes. I. Title.
  F79.6.B76 2012
  974.5—dc23

                                                    2012030448

Printed in the United States of America

10 9 8 7 6 5 4 3 2 1

To Bob Whitcomb, Irving Sheldon, and the rest of the Providence Journal Editorial Department circa 1997, responsible for my own historical event where I first became a professional writer.

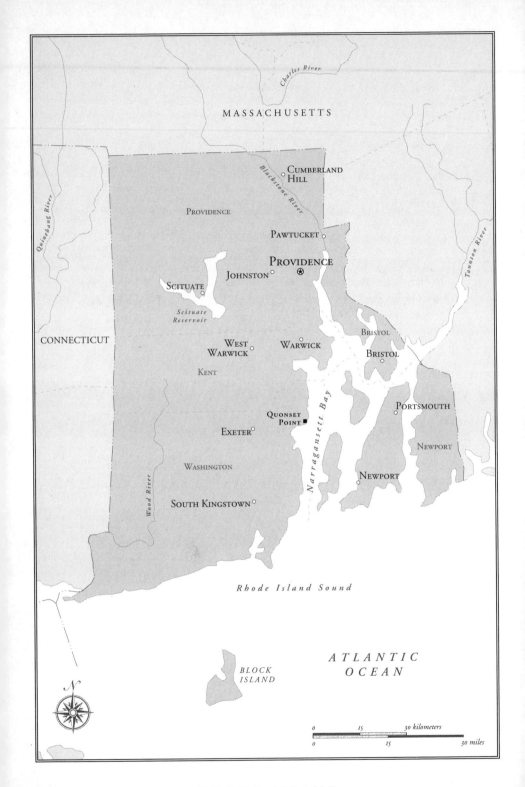

RHODE ISLAND

CONTENTS

Preface vii

The Unsung Settler—1635 1

Keeping a Wife from God—1637 4

The First First Amendment—1638 8

Rhode Island Refuge—1660 13

King Philip's War—1675 17

Burning in Revolution—1772 24

Moses Frees the Slaves—1773 29

Impatient Independence—1776 33

Pirates of the *Providence*—1779 37

Paper Panic—1786 41

The First US Supreme Court Decision—1791 46

Industrial Revolution—1793 50

Arcade at the Mall—1828 56

Dorr to Freedom—1842 60

Powder Burns and Sideburns—1853 65

King of the Court—1881 72

Vampire Consumption—1892 74

Rhode Island's *Titanic*—1907 77

Like Stealing from a Babe—1914 81

The Giant Metal Twinkies That Won the War—1941 84

CONTENTS

Jack and Jackie Get Married—1953 88

Bringing Their A-Game—1964 91

The Times Were A-Changin' for Folk—1965 94

The Great Blizzard—1978 99

Baseball's Longest Game—1981 102

River Relocation—1984 106

Diving DiPrete—1998 109

Burning the House Down—2003 113

The Survivor Goes Down—2005 118

Sock It to Me—2011 121

Rhode Island Facts and Firsts 124

Bibliography 128

Index 131

About the Author 134

PREFACE

I'm still the Rhode Island guy.

It's been some years now since I moved to Massachusetts, but I am still a Rhode Islander, and will undoubtedly remain one for the rest of my life. I still get excited when I hear about Rhode Island on the news, in a way I don't for Massachusetts. No offense, Massachusettsians, but your state is too big for me to feel truly connected to it, even if I do feel like a part of the community in my city.

Rhode Island, on the other hand, is a city-state, like Rome. Founded on seven hills, like Rome, filled with political corruption, like Rome, with a rich history and plenty of good Italian food, like Rome . . . but I digress. I had already written one book about Rhode Island (*Rhode Island Curiosities,* by Globe Pequot Press, filled with things whimsical and weird, and makes a lovely gift for the expatriate Rhode Islander in your life). When I was asked to write another book about Rhode Island, I agreed, even though this book would require much more serious research and be less funny.

I am not a professional historian. In fact, when I was in junior high, I'm pretty sure history was my lowest grade. But I have friends who are historians, translators, and generally scholarly people. I found it valuable to have conversations about what the purpose of history is, whether one can ever talk about "what actually happened," or whether we present a series of different viewpoints and recollections, or one cobbled-together story woven from the threads of the various available accounts.

As for history more directly relevant to the book, I owe thanks to librarians—in this case, a few specific librarians, particularly the fine staff at the East Greenwich Free Library. But I want to extend my thanks generally to all librarians because they are the last bastions of a glorious vision of sharing free knowledge with all citizens. In an age where everything is commodified and public services are increasingly looked upon as expendable, libraries are a bulwark against the destruction of public goods.

A Rhode Island historical tidbit: The Redwood Library and Athenæum, in Newport, is the oldest lending library in America, and the oldest library building in continuous use in the country. It was founded in 1747, based on a mission statement of "having nothing in view but the good of mankind," to make knowledge available to all. Public libraries are a glorious thing, and I trust anyone with an interest in history will likewise see the importance of supporting them.

Dismounting my soapbox, I also owe thanks to two friends of my brother's, Tim Larson and Will Steere, who both are undoubtedly much more historically knowledgeable than I am. Their suggestions for possible topics of research, and a few leads, were quite helpful.

I suppose I should thank my brother Grant as well, since I didn't actually know those guys. And one can't really thank one's brother without thanking one's sister, lest one cause tension at the next family gathering (hi, Halee!). And of course I certainly owe thanks to both of my parents, Jeff and Barbara Brown, not only for their general continued support, but also for their specific support on this project, and constant willingness to drive all over Rhode Island with me whenever I need to do research on a book, and send me information when I do not want to drive all over Rhode Island.

My friends, as always, helped maintain what little remains of my sanity throughout this project, and while they are far too numerous to name individually, I appreciate each one of them no less for that fact. Whether through a good conversation, a long walk, or even just a brief message online to ask how I was doing, my friends offered constant support, for which I am very grateful.

And finally, in terms of constant support, I am incredibly fortunate to have a partner who is the best thing since . . . well, actually just the best thing, bar none. My countless hours of holing up in my office were met with understanding and occasional deliveries of tea and breadstuffs, and basically I feel sorry for everyone who does not live with Debbie.

It remains only for me to thank the staff at Globe Pequot, because even if my editor has been changed at least twice over the course of this project, the fact remains that they asked me to write another book, and then they had to deal with me and my writing. So thanks to whoever drew the short straw.

Oh, and I almost forgot: Thank you for reading. Obviously, a book without a reader is like a tree falling in the forest with nobody around to hear it. Or I guess more accurately, like a tree falling in the forest, being chopped up, then pulped, then pressed into paper, then cut into sheets, then run through a printing press and covered with ink, shipped out to various booksellers, and then having nobody around to hear it.

The point is that history is the entirety of what happened in the past, and without people not only to record it, but also to read it in the present, nobody will know about it in the future. Here assembled are some events that happened in Rhode Island's past, from the first English settler in 1635 to the world's biggest sock, sewn together in 2011.

It is my sincere hope that you enjoy reading about them.

—Seth Brown
North Adams, Massachusetts

THE UNSUNG SETTLER

1635

As most Rhode Islanders know, the state's founder, Roger Williams, was the first European settler to come to Rhode Island. Unfortunately, what most people know tends to be wrong, and this case is no different.

In fact, a year before Roger Williams founded his Providence colony in 1636, a man named William Blackstone arrived in the region of Rhode Island, the first European settler to do so.

But let us start at the beginning. Born to a wealthy landowner and poultryman named Blaxton in England in 1595, William Blaxton earned bachelor's and master's degrees from the Ammanuel College of Cambridge University in 1617 and 1621, respectively. (Blaxton's name was sometimes spelled Blackstone, since people in those days were less picky about spelling.)

Blackstone then was ordained as a clergyman in the Anglican Church. But he was independent and restless, and was known to have frequent disagreements with the Anglican hierarchy. For this reason, he decided to join an expedition in 1623 organized by Sir

Ferdinando Gorges and his council. The Gorges expedition for New England brought Blackstone to the shores of Massachusetts Bay, where he served as chaplain.

Two years later, Robert Gorges (Ferdinando's son) decided to lead the expedition back to England. Blackstone, however, chose to remain, eventually establishing a residence in what is now Boston, on the Shawmut Peninsula near Beacon Hill and Boston Common.

Boston's first English settler stayed there for half a decade until the religiously left-leaning Puritans (who wanted to "purify" the Anglican Church of traces of Roman Catholic "trappings") settled Boston in 1630. As might be expected, Blackstone once again found himself in frequent religious disagreement.

In 1635 the religious differences had become too much to bear, and Blackstone went southwest to what is now the Lonsdale section of Cumberland. There he set up a farm, and a house that he named Study Hill, most likely in honor of the large library that he maintained there to enjoy his solitude. In addition to reading from his library, Blackstone had an interest in horticulture, developing the first American variety of apple. And maintaining his missionary work, Blackstone also preached to the natives and conducted the first Anglican religious services in Rhode Island.

Or technically, the first services in what is now Rhode Island. For the area in which Blackstone settled was originally part of the Plymouth Colony in Massachusetts, and did not become part of Rhode Island during Blackstone's lifetime. Because of this—and perhaps because of Blackstone's reputation for wanting to be left alone—it was Roger Williams who is considered the founder of Rhode Island.

Blackstone met Roger Williams, and after the two became friends, Blackstone would often stop at Williams's home in Cocumscussoc. Blackstone was reportedly beloved by the children, to whom he used to bring sweet apples from his orchard at Study Hill. Previous to this, some of them had never seen an apple.

Cocumscussoc was a convenient stop on Blackstone's frequent sojourns to Providence to buy more books for his library. Blackstone was known to travel atop a large white bull.

Aside from new books and a few miscellaneous supplies, Blackstone had most everything he needed at Study Hill: milk and meat from his herds, fish from the river, game from the forest, and grain, fruit, and vegetables from his gardens, orchards, and fields.

In 1659, at the age of sixty-four, Blackstone returned to Boston, where he married a widow named Sarah Stevenson, who bore him one son, named John. William Blackstone died in 1675, which mercifully saved him from seeing King Philip's War ravage the land a few weeks later, and specifically spared him from seeing his beloved house and library burned to ashes.

It would not be until over three score years later in the 1740s that Rhode Island annexed the Cumberland area, thus retroactively making William Blackstone the first English settler to come to what is now Rhode Island.

A large granite monument in Broad Street, in Cumberland, now bears his name, as does the Blackstone River valley.

KEEPING A WIFE FROM GOD

1637

The year 1637 was when possibly the first recorded reprimand of a husband for abusing his wife occurred. It was also the date of a battle over a woman's soul. Particularly, the soul of one Mrs. Jane Verin. (Some sources have referred to Mrs. Verin with the name Mary or Ann, but it is believed that her correct name is Jane.)

Roger Williams was part of the Antinomians (literally, "against the law"), attracted to some tenets of the faith, such as separation of church and state, and opposed to the taking of oaths and bearing of arms. The Antinomians believed that rebaptism was necessary to formally sever all ties to the Bay Colony church. (Without this rebaptism, it was believed that Antinomians would technically remain members of the old church.)

Williams began holding frequent Antinomian religious services in his home. Jane Verin was one of the adherents of Williams at the time, and her joining with the Antinomians became an issue for her husband, Joshua Verin. Joshua was bothered that his wife was frequently away from home, and forbade her to attend future services with Williams. Joshua had beaten Jane Verin until "she went in danger of life" to prevent her from attending services.

Mrs. Verin might well have been disappointed to have been kept from church, since it was one of the few places in those days where women had any kind of position. Church was a rare place where wives could earn membership (albeit not govern), hear sermons supporting their guardianship of sexual mores, and be in an environment that elevated charity over commerce and neighborliness over trade. As the rare place where women could actually meet as people and socialize with neighbors, church may well have been prized by Mrs. Verin.

Thus, it must have been doubly disturbing for her to have been beaten to prevent her from attending. The result of this was perhaps the first officially recorded disapproval of a husband for abusing his wife. On May 21, 1637, Joshua Verin was censured by formal vote of his townsmen for "endangering his wife," Jane, by virtue of denying her the right to attend religious services with the frequency required. Jane had desired to attend Roger Williams's meetings "as often as called for," but Joshua Verin did not like the Antinomian discourses forwarded by Roger Williams, and said, "She shall not."

The result was what historical record describes as a highly spirited court hearing. William Arnold, one of the first settlers of Providence and a notorious devil's advocate against Williams, pointed out that while Roger Williams had declared that "no man would be molested for his conscience" in Rhode Island, this declaration said nothing about women. Furthermore, argued Arnold, such a declaration could not possibly apply to wives and children because it would breach God's law that subjected them to the will of their husbands and fathers, respectively. The supreme rule accorded to the man of the house was a common belief at the time.

The writings of John Winthrop describe Arnold as "a witty man," leading some to believe that Arnold did not intend his comment seriously. But the issue of whether abusing one's wife to keep her from ungodliness could be considered an "act of conscience" was not at all settled.

Mr. John Greene, one of the original proprieters of Providence, however, declared that if they should so restrain wives, "all the women in the country would cry out of them." Others present said that "if Verin would not suffer his wife to have her libertie, the church should dispose her to some other man, who would use her better." Arnold concluded that whatever Verin did, he did out of conscience, and no man should be censured for that.

Joshua himself argued that he was not restricting his wife's religious liberty, but rather was trying to ensure that she lived in conformity to God's law—which in this case meant submission to her husband. His neighbors, he argued, should stop meddling in his affairs and allow him to live in the manner that God intended.

Yet the townsmen agreed that if Jane Verin, after faithfully discharging all her duties as a wife and mother, felt conscience-bound to attend Roger Williams's meetings, then she should be allowed to do so. In the end, it was decided that Joshua Verin had breached a covenant for restraining the "libertie of conscience," and consequently should be "withheld from the libertie of voting till he shall declare the contrarie."

At the time, Joshua owned property next door to Williams on Towne Street. Some continued to argue that his right to conscience was being breached because he did not want to attend religious services, and didn't want his wife to do so either.

On May 22, just after the censure vote, Roger Williams wrote to Governor John Winthrop suggesting that the issue was not religion, but abuse:

Sir, we have bene long afflicted by a young man, boys-terous and desperate, Philip Verin's sonn of Salem, who as he hath refused to heare the word with us this twelve month, so because he could not draw his wife, a gracious and modest woman, to the same ungodliness brutishly, which she and we long bearing, though with his furious blows she went in danger of life, at the last the major vote of us discard him from our civil freedom, or dis-franchize, etc.; he will have justice (as he clamours) at other courts; I wish he might, for a foule and slanderous and brutish carriage, wch God hath delivered him up unto, he will hale his wife with ropes to Salem, where she must needes be troubled and troublesom as difference yet stand. She is willing to stay and live with him or elsewhere where she may not offend etc. I shall humbly request that this item be accepted and he no way counte-nanced until (if need be) I further trouble you.

For indeed, Joshua Verin was not well pleased with the censure, and rather than comply with the terms thereof (either remaining without the vote, or declaring that he had changed his mind), he decided to flee to Salem. He still had family in Salem who had become leading citizens in his absence, and so he was happy to return to his father and brother.

Joshua's wife was, as Williams mentioned in his letter to Governor Winthrop, dragged along with Joshua when he left Providence. Mrs. Verin was not heard from again. Years later, in 1650, Joshua Verin wrote to Providence demanding compensation for the home lot and other property that was formerly his, but there is no indication that he ever returned to present his case in person, which was required as a bare minimum to have a potentially valid claim, let alone to collect on it.

THE FIRST FIRST AMENDMENT

1638

Roger Williams brought religious freedom to America.

Perhaps you are thinking, "But wasn't America founded by a group of Puritans who came here seeking religious freedom?" Well, no, mainly they came here seeking religious Puritanism. Freedom is something else entirely, as Roger Williams would learn.

But let us start at the beginning. Roger Williams was born in London, the son of successful London merchant tailor James Williams and Alice Pemberton. His youth was spent in the parish of St. Sepulchre's, near Newgate in London. There he doubtless became aware of the events that had occurred at nearby Smithfield, where heretics and Puritans were often burned at the stake. Some historians theorize that this influenced his strong beliefs in religious freedom.

As a teenager, Roger Williams became acquainted with Sir Edward Coke, a jurist, lawyer, and former chief justice of England. Coke took on Williams as an apprentice, enrolling him at Charter House, and then at Pembroke College at Cambridge University. At

Pembroke he excelled in many languages, ranging from Latin to Hebrew, and received scholarships for his work.

Williams had taken Holy Orders in the Church of England, but during his stay at Cambridge, he broke with the Anglican state church and joined the Puritans instead—to the dismay of his parents. Puritans initially aimed to "purify" the Anglican Church from within, but Williams was moving toward separatism. He had become a Puritan at Cambridge, forfeiting any chance at a place of preferment in the Anglican Church. After graduating from Cambridge in 1627, Williams became the chaplain to a wealthy Puritan family led by Sir William Macham.

Two years later, Williams married Mary Barnard at the Church of High Laver, in Essex. But his dissatisfaction with high church politics—especially as practiced by the Archbishop of Canterbury, William Laud—made it all but impossible for Williams to remain in England, especially given his controversial ideas about freedom of worship. Williams believed the Church of England to be corrupt and false, and slowly but surely was becoming a separatist.

So it was that in late 1630, a mere decade after the Pilgrims had landed at Plymouth, Roger Williams and Mary boarded the ship *Lyon* bound for Massachusetts Bay. They arrived in 1631, at which point Williams was quickly invited to become an assistant minister in the Boston Church.

Williams, however, refused, adamantly unwilling to join a church that still had ties to the Church of England. His separatist beliefs required him to break off from the Church of England to find a pure worship of God. Williams also believed that civil magistrates should be unable to punish people for breaking religious laws (such as blasphemy or breaking the Sabbath), and that everyone had a right to religious freedom.

This belief system, naturally, was incompatible with the Church of England. But the principles that Williams espoused upon his arrival in America were the same ones for which he would become famous: separatism, freedom of religion, and separation of church and state.

With no Congregational or Baptist church available that would tolerate such beliefs, Williams eventually found a church in Salem with separatist leanings. This church had invited him to be an assistant minister, and then pastor. Williams moved to Plymouth and began preaching there, where his teachings seemed to meet with approval.

But Williams grew discontent that the Plymouth church was not sufficiently separated from the Church of England. No matter where he went, his preaching continued to be controversial. It didn't help that he questioned the very right of the colonists to take the Indians' land away from them based on the flimsy legality of the royal charter.

Unsurprisingly, such talk did not endear Williams to the powers at large in Massachusetts at the time. Governor William Bradford wrote that Williams fell "into some strange opinions which caused some controversy between the church and him." Strange or not, Williams condemned the royal charters and believed that the colonists had no right to take Indian land unless it was paid for.

He moved back to Salem in 1633, but no matter where he went, Roger Williams spoke his mind, which did not agree with the ruling Puritans. Authorities summoned him to the General Court, furious that he had written a tract attacking the royal charters. The tract disappeared, but Williams was allowed to stay in Massachusetts since he promised not to discuss the charter's legality ever again.

As pastor of the church in Salem, Williams questioned the legality of the royal charter again, declaring that the king's authority to grant control was based on a "solemn public lie." In 1635 he was ordered back to the General Court to account for himself. Repeatedly. Whether for attacking the charter or for opposing the new oath of allegiance to the colonial government, Williams was branded a troublemaker. The court held power over the town of Salem and used Williams as a negotiation point.

Finally, the dam broke. Williams would be suffered no more. Late in the year, he was tried by the General Court and found guilty of spreading "new authority of magistrates" and "diverse, new, and dangerous opinions." He was convicted of heresy and ordered banished from the colony.

However, by the time they came around to deport him in January 1636, Roger Williams had already fled southwest to the current Narragansett Bay, on the advice of John Winthrop. There he became friendly with local Indians, such as the Wampanoag and their sachem Massasoit. Williams was impressed by Native American hospitality, writing, "I known them to leave their house and mat to lodge a friend or stranger, When Jews and Christians oft have sent Christ Jesus to the Manger."

Williams then purchased (rather than claimed by charter) land from the Narragansett chiefs Canonicus and Miantonomi. Williams considered the land "a sense of god's merciful providence unto me in my distress," and named the new land Providence.

In 1638 Williams had established a plantation based on complete religious liberty and separation of church and state. He strongly believed that freedom of conscience, liberty of the soul, was a gift from God and that all humans had a right to religious freedom—even women and Indians.

To safeguard this religious freedom, Williams believed a "wall of separation" was required between the "Garden of Christ" and the "Wilderness of the World." He was the first to espouse this belief in the separation of church and state, a foundational idea to the Constitution and First Amendment. He published many tracts related to the idea of religious freedom, including "The Bloody Tenent of Persecution for Cause of Conscience" and "A Plea for Religious Liberty."

Roger Williams believed that no political arrangement can be legitimized by scripture, that there is no civil power to enforce religion. Puritans believed they enforced ten commandments, whereas Roger Williams said the first table (the commandments regarding God worship) had been set by Jesus as a matter for the spirit realm.

Thus, he believed the state was unjustified in controlling religious belief. Rhode Island was the first commonwealth to make religious freedom a main principle, separating church and state. All of Rhode Island's founding documents enshrine Williams's beliefs. The Royal Charter of 1663 granted "full liberty in religious concernments," stating that "noe person within the sayd colonye, at any time hereafter, shall bee any wise molested, punished, disquieted, or called in question for any differences in opinione in matters of religion."

Thus was Rhode Island founded as a haven for religious freedom, the legacy of Roger Williams.

RHODE ISLAND REFUGE

1660

Imagine a game of tag where Boston religious authorities are "It," the penalty for being caught is hanging, and the "safe base" is Rhode Island. That roughly sums up the death of Mary (Barrett) Dyer.

Originally born Mary Barrett in 1610, in 1633 she married William Dyer of Somersetshire, England. This was good fortune for Mr. Dyer, as Mary was generally well thought of. Massachusetts Governor John Winthrop described her as "a very proper and fair woman." Dutch writer Gerald Crosse called her "a person of no mean extraction and parentage, of an estate pretty plentiful, of a comely stature and countenance, of a piercing knowledge in many things, of a wonderfully sweet and pleasant disposition, so fit for great affairs that she wanted nothing that was manly except only the name and sex."

In other words, Mary Dyer not only was pretty and charming, but also had all the education and standing to do important things like the menfolk did. With this education, Mary Dyer and her husband supported Antinomians such as Anne Hutchinson and John Wheelwright in Boston. And this, in turn, caused some less complimentary quotes from the orthodox Puritans who ran most of the town at that time.

The Puritans considered Dyer and Hutchinson part of an "Antinomian heresy," since the women were organizing groups to study the Bible who believed they could directly receive God's grace through faith, rather than earning salvation through good works and the established hierarchy of clergy.

In late 1637 William Dyer was disenfranchised and then disarmed for supporting another Antinomian named John Wheelwright. At around the same time, Mary Dyer secretly gave birth to a stillborn child, delivered by Anne Hutchinson and buried privately.

Hutchinson continued preaching against the rest of the local clergy, and so she was eventually expelled from the Puritan Church. Mary Dyer left the church in a show of support. And when Hutchinson was banished from Massachusetts, so too went the Dyers, ever stalwart. They moved to Rhode Island to escape the hostile atmosphere of the Massachusetts Bay Colony.

In 1638 William Dyer became one of the founders of Portsmouth as a signer of the Portsmouth Compact. At roughly the same time, Mary Dyer's dead baby was exhumed on the authority of Governor Winthrop. Since Anne Hutchinson had assisted in the delivery, Winthrop claimed that this "monster" was evidence of heresy.

After a decade on Aquidneck Island, Mary Dyer left her husband and six kids in the winter of 1650 to sail to England. She was fascinated with George Fox's seekers, an independent group who believed the Christian church had lost its way and thus rejected regular churches to claim religious liberty. George Fox soon formed the Quakers (Society of Friends). Antinomian and Quaker beliefs were very similar, plus Quakerism was the only faith that recognized women in the ministry from the start, so Dyer quickly became a Quaker.

Mary Dyer remained in England until 1657, when she set sail for home. However, as she passed through Boston on the way to Rhode Island, she was arrested and imprisoned for heresy, as Quakerism was not looked on kindly. After she had been imprisoned for two months, William Dyer convinced Governor John Endicott to release his wife by agreeing she would never return to Massachusetts.

Mary Dyer returned to the family farm, now grown (as were her children), but she was restless. Her family had done fine with her away, and she was not cut out to play housewife. She continued preaching as a Quaker missionary, leading to her expulsion in 1658 from the Puritan colony of New Haven.

Dyer returned to the safe haven of Rhode Island, but in 1659 she heard that many of her friends (and Friends), such as Christopher Holder of Providence, were in prison in Boston. Holder, a Quaker preacher who had previously been jailed and sent back to England, had been arrested and banished to Rhode Island but was back preaching in Salem. Even after being attacked there, the next day he went to preach in Boston, where he was arrested and whipped.

Mary Dyer visited on a mission of mercy to Boston to protest the imprisonment and to comfort the jailed Quakers. But she'd been previously banished, so she was seized and sentenced to hang. Her husband wrote a letter asking for kinder treatment, but this time his pleas fell on deaf ears. Mary was upon the gallows and about to be hanged with two other Quakers.

Suddenly her son galloped in on horseback. As captain of a coasting vessel, he had petitioned for her reprieve, and Governor Endicott had granted it. Dyer was told to step down from the gallows, but she replied, "She was there willing to suffer as her Brethren did, unless they would null their wicked Law, she had no freedom to accept their reprieve."

In fact, she had no freedom not to; Dyer was forced down from the gallows and onto a horse, and escorted back to the safety of Rhode Island once again.

After teaching religion to the people around her for several months (including slaves and Indians, a rarity at the time), Mary Dyer read a secondhand account of her near-hanging, saying she had meekly accepted her life and promised never to return. This so angered her, she went to Boston again in April 1660 to protest. She was, unsurprisingly, imprisoned and condemned.

Her husband wrote a letter of plea to Governor Endicott, but by then nothing could stop Mary's martyrdom wish. When asked if she would behave if she were allowed to live, she said, "Nay, I cannot; for in obedience to the will of the Lord God I came, and in His will I abide faithful to the death."

Dyer was stubborn and strong in her beliefs. She was hung on Boston Common on June 1, 1660, at age forty-nine. If only she had made it back once more to the safe haven of Rhode Island.

KING PHILIP'S WAR

1675

King Philip (also called Metacom or Metacomet) was the son of Massasoit, the great sachem of the Wampanoag. They'd once been subordinate to the Narragansett. Massasoit had always been friendly with colonists and it had made the tribe strong, providing them a defense against their traditional enemies, such as the Mohegan. Massasoit's alliance provided the Wampanoag with not only a threatening ally against potential attacks from other tribes, but also a trade partner.

However, the colonists frequently encroached upon native land, and relations between the colonists and the tribe became increasingly strained. Metacomet resented the constant encroachment of white settlers onto his father's land, "forcing them further and further back into their hunting grounds."

It didn't help that Philip had seen many atrocities committed by white colonists. A hunter had captured a squaw and ordered her "torn to pieces by his dogs. . . . Bounties were placed upon the heads of all young and defenseless redmen, $130 being paid for the scalp of an Indian boy, $50 for that of a squaw."

Still, when he first took leadership of the Wampanoag, Metacomet (Philip) made many concessions to the Plymouth Colony (although he did irritate Plymouth officials by giving preference to Rhode Island settlers when selling Wampanoag land). Philip's father, Massasoit, died in 1661, and Philip's brother Wamsutta died in 1662, the latter of which occurred under suspicious circumstances that led some to suspect the colonists. (After Massasoit died, the colonists suspected a plot against them and ordered Wamsutta to Plymouth. On the way home Wamsutta became seriously ill and died. The Wampanoag were told he died of fever, but many Indians—including Philip—thought he had been poisoned.)

Philip became sachem of the Pokanoket and grand sachem of the Wampanoag Confederacy in 1662, after the death of his two family members. And while Massasoit had been favorably disposed toward the colonists, Metacomet distrusted them. Metacomet began negotiating with the other Native American tribes, rather than the Plymouth Colony.

Massasoit had been one of the chief enablers of the Plymouth Colony for many years, but Metacomet resented their increasing encroachment upon his tribal lands and chose not to honor his father's policy of appeasement. Metacomet began reaching out to other tribes, asking for their support in the war he saw as inevitable.

"Brothers, these people from the unknown world will cut down our groves, spoil our hunting and planting grounds, and drive us and our children from the graves of our fathers," he is rumored to have said.

Under Metacomet's leadership, skirmishes had been breaking out. Colonists said that Metacom had "gathered together all his allies among the brow-beated tribes and struck blow after blow on the English settlements," to "pounce upon unprotected farm-houses, burn, plunder, murder, and then disappear into the forest."

The Dutch had continued selling guns to the Indians, and violence only escalated. By 1675 things had come to a head, and some of the violent confrontations finally spurred on a full-scale war.

One of Metacom's advisers, Sassamon, spread a rumor to Plymouth Colony officials that Metacom was planning attacks on various colonial settlements. In March 1675 Metacom was brought in front of a public court, and although the court admitted that it had no proof other than a rumor, Metacom was warned that any further reports would have harsh consequences for the Wampanoag.

A week later Sassamon's murdered body was found in ice-covered Assawompset Pond, allegedly killed by a few of Philip's Wampanoag, angry at his betrayal. On the testimony of a Christian Native American witness, Plymouth Colony officials arrested three Wampanoag, including one of Metacom's counselors.

After a trial by a jury of twelve Englishmen and six pro-English Native Americans (or "Christian Indians"), the three Wampanoag men were hanged in June 1675. Some Wampanoag believed that both the trial and the court's sentence infringed on Wampanoag sovereignty. This execution, combined with the rumors that the English wanted to capture Metacomet, was enough to start a war.

Metacom called together a council of war on Mount Hope, and most Wampanoag were firmly behind him, with the exception of the Nauset on Cape Cod and the small groups on the offshore islands. Many allies were ready to follow Metacom as well, including the Nipmucks, Pocomtucs, and some Pennacooks and Eastern Abenakis from farther north.

However, not all Indians fell in line with Metacom. The Narragansett remained neutral at the beginning of the war. And many Christian Indians had offered to fight against Metacom and his allies, serving as warriors, scouts, advisers, and spies. But the English prejudice against Native Americans was difficult to overcome. Furthermore, many believed that all Christian Indians were secretly spies for Metacom, and thus many Christian Indians were collectively moved by the Massachusetts government to Deer Island in Boston Harbor.

Roger Williams attempted to negotiate a treaty with the Wampanoag, but his friends among the tribes (such as Massasoit) were all dead. His overtures of peace failed, and the first Indian attack would come in June 1675. A band of Pokanoket attacked the settlement of Swansea in Plymouth Colony, laying siege to the town and eventually destroying it. Although the battle took place in Plymouth, the injured Indians fled to Rhode Island.

However, once they reached Rhode Island, they were well treated. Historical records note that the old men, women, children, and the wounded and feeble members of the tribes whose warriors had fought for King Philip, had all come to Rhode Island seeking refuge from the Narragansett chiefs and their people. In spite of the war, these displaced peoples of the enemy were treated kindly. The noncombatants of the opposing tribes were fed and clothed, and the sick and wounded were nursed back to health and their wounds carefully attended to.

Meanwhile, Plymouth responded with swift force, sending out a military expedition only a few days later to destroy the Wampanoag town at Mount Hope. This in turn brought more attacks from the Native Americans, attacking Middleborough, Dartmouth, and Mendon in July, Brookfield and Lancaster in August, and Deerfield, Hadley, and Northfield in September.

This finally caused the New England Confederation to officially declare war on the Native Americans in September 1675. In October a large attack against the Springfield settlement took place, burning most of the town to the ground. Infuriated, the United Colonies of New England then demanded that the Narragansett (who had retained neutrality in this conflict) surrender all of the Wampanoag to them. The Narragansett, though still neutral, had no desire to turn over the injured Native Americans to the hands of the colonists. Once they had made clear their intentions not to surrender King Philip, the colonies declared war on the Narragansett in November 1675. Thus the Narragansett neutrality and avoidance of the war came to an end.

Josiah Winslow, governor of the Plymouth Colony, led an attack against the Narragansett. His forces rampaged through Rhode Island, burning several towns known to be occupied by Narragansett. The Narragansett, aware of the attacks, had mostly fled and retreated to a giant fort covering nearly five acres, hidden in the middle of a swamp.

A thousand well-armed white troops reached the village of Wickford, Rhode Island, "bent on seeking out the Indian stronghold somewhere in that vicinity." They suspected Philip was sheltered there, and led by an Indian guide, on December 19, 1675, the colonial force found the Narragansett fort near present-day South Kingstown.

The head sachem, Canonchet, refused to surrender King Philip, and so the colonists attacked the Indian fort. A combined force of Plymouth, Massachusetts, and Connecticut militia numbering about 1,000 men, including about 150 Pequots and Mohegans, attacked the fort. The battle that followed was known as the Great Swamp Fight or the Great Swamp Massacre. The militia killed many Narragansett and then burned the fort.

Historical records confirm the horror of the event. After a few hours of fighting, the raiders had set a hedge on fire. The flames soon spread to the entire encampment, and many were caught in burning wigwams, screaming for mercy that would not be granted. The Swamp Massacre was like a scene from a horror film, and by the time the flames died down, sources estimate that 300 Indian warriors were killed in that battle, and 400 women and children were killed. Nearly 450 Indians were taken prisoner as well.

A few of the Indians escaped into the frozen swamp, but with their home and food stores destroyed, winter offered no respite. On the other hand, the Great Swamp Fight was not without losses for the colonists. Roughly seventy colonists were killed in the assault, and many more died on the trip back to Wickford, victims of their injuries or the exhaustion of marching through a harsh winter landscape.

But the blow against the Narragansett was a decisive one.

In March 1676 the tribes launched a last-ditch attack against Plymouth Plantation. The town survived the assault, but the natives had proved that they could successfully attack colonial territory, and assaulted Longmeadow, Marlborough, and Simsbury, capturing and torturing several colonials. Later in March the natives simultaneously struck out against Providence and Springfield, burning both.

Pawtuxet was raided, and the animals were all driven off. Houses were burned near Wickford. Warwick was nearly destroyed, with most citizens fleeing. In Providence only twenty-seven of five hundred men stayed, but could not prevent twenty-nine houses being from burned. Many of Rhode Island's homes were burned to the ground.

Roger Williams was sad, saying to the Indians, "In this Hous of mine now burning before mine Eyes hath Lodged kindly Some Thousands of You these Ten Years." Roger Williams said in a letter to his brother, "They knew many times I had Quenched fires between the Bay and them, and Plimoath, and Quiniticutt, and them."

However, this was the final turning point of the war. Although the colonists had to retreat to the larger towns, in those larger towns the colonists had a plentitude of cultivated cropland. The natives, meanwhile, were running low on supplies. They had hoped for some assistance from the Canadian French, but none came. Connecticut's Mohegan and Pequot tribes allied with the colonists, and the Mohawks rejected King Philip's offer of an alliance. The result was a Wampanoag tribe under attack not only by colonists, but by other Indian tribes as well.

In April 1676 the Narragansett were defeated and their great sachem, Canonchet, was killed. In May, Captain William Turner of the Massachusetts militia and 150 volunteers attacked a large Native American fishing camp. In June the colonists were joined by some Mohegan allies in a fight at Hadley. Repeatedly colonists and Indian allies were routing the remaining Wampanoag and Narragansett forces.

The colonists promised mercy to those who surrendered, and thus Philip's allies began to desert him. By early July more than four hundred had surrendered to the colonists.

Major Benjamin Church and Captain Josiah Standish of the Plymouth Colony militia led a company of Puritan rangers and Native American allies that finally hunted down and ambushed King Philip on August 12, 1676. At Mount Hope, in Rhode Island, a Pocasset Indian named John Alderman shot and killed King Philip. Metacom was beheaded, and his body was "drawn and quartered and his head placed above the stockade at Plymouth as a warning to other potential rebels."

Metacom's death marked the end of King Philip's War. Philip's few remaining followers were killed or sold as slaves. Most captured Indians were sold into slavery in Cadiz or the West Indies. Roger Williams sought compassion, saying, "The most High delights in mercy," asking colonists to treat slaves "to make mercy eminent" (although he had approved their sale, so obviously Williams was okay with slavery as a concept).

The Narragansett and Wampanoag who escaped death sought refuge with Niantics who had not joined the war. This group together became the Narragansett.

The devastation King Philip's War had caused was unmatched. More than six hundred colonists and three thousand Native Americans had died. Nearly half of the region's towns were destroyed, and more than half had been attacked; the local economy was all but ruined. Things looked grim for the colonists, but aided by a robust population growth rate, they managed to rebuild their towns and continued to thrive.

Still, King Philip's War remains one of the most destructive conflicts in North America's history, by sheer percentage of population devastated by the war.

BURNING IN REVOLUTION

1772

The Boston Tea Party had better marketing.

Schoolchildren across America have been taught that the Boston Tea Party was the big kickoff to the American Revolution that led to this country's independence. Elementary schools have taken great pains to communicate that a bunch of rebels, dressed as Indians, dumping tea into the harbor, sparked the revolution. Like many things one may have learned in history class as a kid, this is incorrect.

In fact, the first act of war against the British during the Revolutionary War took place in Newport, Rhode Island, with the burning of the British customs schooner the HMS *Gaspee.*

In March 1772 British Navy Lieutenant William Dudingston was sent to Narragansett Bay to enforce the Stamp Act. Dudingston was, in a word, disliked, by smugglers and colonists alike. Part of this may have been due to Dudingston's insolent and overbearing personal nature. But most of it was likely because Dudingston had a penchant for harassing and stopping colonial ships—even those that had already been cleared by customs.

Dudingston commanded the HMS *Gaspee,* an eight-gun schooner stationed at Newport to prevent any ships from landing that had not paid sufficient duties. And with the *Gaspee,* he stopped and boarded all ships both entering and leaving Rhode Island, regardless of whether they had been through customs. He stopped ships traveling between Newport and Providence. He generally sailed up and down the bay, hailing boats and then immediately firing a warning shot across their bows if they did not stop and wait to be searched. Accounts from the time suggest that Dudingston would always ask for an additional payment of taxes, regardless of what customs duties had been paid.

On June 9, 1772, at around noon, Captain Benjamin Lindsey set out from Newport, captaining the sloop *Hannah.* He had already passed through customs at Newport and had no desire to be stopped, searched, and retaxed. So, with the wind at the north and his sails spread, he headed out of the harbor and decided to flee from Dudingston.

As expected, it was not long before the *Gaspee* appeared in pursuit. The customary shot was fired across the *Hannah's* bow as a warning to stop, but Captain Lindsey ignored it and maintained his course, causing the *Gaspee* to continue giving chase. This kept up for several miles, up to Namquid Point a few miles below Providence, where Lindsey led his little packet over a sandbar.

Dudingston, who was both less familiar with the local waters and captaining a much larger ship, ran aground. The schooner was grounded, stuck in the sand, and unlikely to be freed anytime soon.

Lindsey, meanwhile, wasted no time. Having arrived safely in Providence at around sunset, he immediately sought out John Brown, who was not only Lindsey's employer but also one of Rhode Island's most powerful citizens at the time. Brown reached the conclusion that the *Gaspee* was going to be stuck until after midnight and that an opportunity had thus arisen to take action to end Dudingston's reign of terror on Rhode Island waters.

Brown quickly assembled a meeting of "concerned citizens" at Sabin's Tavern for further discussion. Assemble they did, and Brown directed one of his shipmasters to gather eight longboats from the harbor and move them to Fenner's Wharf, just across from Mr. James Sabin's house. He also ordered that the oars and rowlocks be muffled to prevent any suspicious noise.

Brown then sent out a town crier, announcing that the *Gaspee* was going to be grounded until at least 3 a.m., and that anyone who "felt a disposition to go and destroy that troublesome vessel" should meet at Sabin's house. Numerous people gathered there, casting bullets in the kitchen and making plans.

At around ten o'clock, the order was given to cross the street to Fenner's Wharf and embark. Each boat was led by a captain, and the captains were led by Captain Abraham Whipple. Under cover of darkness, the eight boats rowed toward the *Gaspee*. Down they went past Fox Point, around Field's Point, and onto the very sandbar where the *Gaspee* lay. They approached very close to the schooner before the watch on deck discovered their presence.

Finally, at sixty yards away, a sentinel suddenly spotted the boats and called out, "Who comes there?" No answer. The sentinel called out once more, but no reply was given from the boats. Soon Lieutenant Dudingston himself appeared on the starboard deck and called out, "Who comes there?" Still no answer. But when Dudingston called out his challenge once more, Captain Whipple had a reply:

"I am the sheriff of the County of Kent, God damn you! I have got a warrant to apprehend you, God damn you; so surrender, God damn you!"

As Whipple was yelling all of this, young Joseph Bucklin decided to take matters into his own hands and fired his musket, hitting

Dudingston in the groin and knocking him over. "I have killed the rascal," exclaimed Bucklin, although this would later prove to be false.

The attackers then swarmed the HMS *Gaspee,* and by sheer numbers and hand-to-hand fighting, drove the crew below. John Brown took control of the ship, and the commander and crew were all taken prisoner. At dawn the order was given to put the prisoners onto the boats and have them rowed ashore at Warwick and then taken to Pawtuxet.

Meanwhile, the *Gaspee* was ransacked for official documents. All of the letters, papers, and records were collected and given to John Brown. All but one of the longboats were ordered to depart, leaving only the leaders of the expedition. When the longboats returned, John Brown's men had put torch to the vessel, setting the *Gaspee* aflame. The ship burned, fires leaping from the deck, up the masts through the sails and rigging, as boats full of Rhode Islanders silently watched the flames grow higher.

Suddenly there was a huge explosion, followed by a few smaller ones. The flames had reached the *Gaspee's* powder magazines, and burning debris was flung high into the air as the boats were shaken by the dull roar of the explosion. The *Gaspee* was destroyed, and the first blow against British despotism had been struck.

The *Gaspee* Affair, as it came to be known, of course did not end there. The colonists had struck a blow against the British Empire, which tended not to look kindly upon piracy and treason. Fear of British retribution abounded, with colonists worried that the English government might declare martial law, send in troops to occupy Newport and Providence, or simply revoke the colony's charter.

King George III and his ministers appointed a commission to investigate and arrest any suspected inhabitants of the colony who might have been involved in destroying the *Gaspee.* Thankfully for the colonists, the commission was headed by Governor Joseph

Wanton, who was not only a Rhode Islander, but also a good friend of John Brown's.

The British government offered substantial rewards for anyone who could provide the identities of the perpetrators. A man named Aaron Briggs, the indentured servant of Samuel Tompkins of Prudence Island, ran away from his master and sought refuge on the revenue schooner *Beaver*. One of the *Gaspee*'s former crewmen recognized Briggs from the night of the fire and notified the commander.

On being questioned, Briggs admitted that he had taken part in the attack, and implicated various men of high standing in the colony, including none other than John Brown himself. Subpoenas were sent out to many Rhode Island officials and to all the men Briggs had named as party to the burning of the *Gaspee*.

The officials were quick to express their disapproval at the lawless acts of the "unknown" miscreants while declaring their utmost devotion to the "good King George" and the laws of England. Conveniently, while busy condemning the illegal acts of the "unknown and rebellious attackers," they were also all too busy to appear in person before the commissioners.

On June 23, 1773, the commission closed its investigation. Their final report to the king stated that the *Gaspee* had been destroyed by "persons unknown." They accused Captain John Linzee of obtaining Aaron Briggs's confession by illegal threats of hanging.

Despite the king of England's $5,000 reward for the leader of the expedition, and the $2,500 reward for the arrest of any of the men who had been with him, nobody was ever outed to the Crown. While most of the town knew exactly who had been on the *Gaspee* that night, they were not about to betray their compatriots. Or perhaps, simply, patriots, who had delivered their colony from the hated *Gaspee* and struck the first blow of revolution against Britain.

MOSES FREES THE SLAVES

1773

When people hear the name of Moses, they think of a man helping to lead slaves to freedom. This is the case not only with the biblical Moses, but also with one of Rhode Island's famous folks, Moses Brown.

Moses Brown was born in 1738 to Hope Power and Captain James Brown, a direct descendant of Chad Brown, who was one of the original founders of Providence along with Roger Williams. Moses had four brothers, John, Joseph, Nicholas, and James. At the time of his birth, it would be hard to imagine that Moses Brown would grow up to be a reformer and help free slaves. After all, many of Rhode Island's prominent citizens had gotten rich on the back of the slave trade, and the Brown family was no exception.

Not only did the slave traders themselves profit, but all of the auxiliary industries benefited as well, from shipbuilders and tar producers, to textile manufacturers or anyone who used cotton picked from the plantations of the South.

Truth be told, though, the Brown family couldn't even claim to have only auxiliary involvement. They were directly involved with slavery, not only owning slaves of their own, but also participating heavily in the slave trade themselves.

The most well-documented example of this is the ill-fated voyage of the slave ship *Sally,* a brig that had traveled to Guinea in 1764. The ship was obviously outfitted for slave trafficking, with forty handcuffs, three chains, many shackles, and so on. The logs kept by Captain Esek Hopkins detail how the slaves were traded for various other goods and possessions.

From the ship's logs:

- "4 slaves 2 men 2 women" traded for 270 iron bars

- "a Small garle Slave" for 4 bars

- "4 Slaves 2 old woman & 2 old man" for 240 bars

- Other slaves lost by death, with one woman "hanged her Self between Decks"

The captain's logs also reveal that the captured Africans did not come along easily. A revolt rose up among the captured slaves, who were also sickened by the plague that broke out. Hopkins may well have regretted trading his simple cargo of rum for a ship full of unrest and death. Many of the slaves died of the plague, and many more killed themselves, with the result that only twenty-four slaves made it back in sufficiently good condition to be sold.

This, of course, was seen as the main tragedy of the event by most of the Brown family. It was an unmitigated financial disaster for Nicholas Brown and company, considered by many to have been the worst voyage ever undertaken from Providence.

The Brown brothers were apparently rich enough to weather the storm, regretting the financial loss but glad to know the captain was still in good health. Only Moses was bothered by the numerous deaths themselves, haunted by the disaster for the captured Africans.

Still, that was to be the last slave trade of Moses's brothers Nick and Joe. Sadly, Moses's brother John Brown had no such compunctions and continued to be involved with the slave trade for many more years—even after it became officially illegal. In 1800 John Brown was one of only five congressmen to speak against a bill to reinforce the federal statute of 1794 prohibiting citizen participation in the foreign slave trade.

However, Moses Brown was horrified by the event that began to change his position on slavery. In 1764 he married his cousin Anna, daughter of his uncle Obadiah. That same year Moses became deputy of the General Assembly, working as a political ally of Governor Stephen Hopkins.

Less than a decade later, in 1773, Moses Brown's wife, Anna, died. She was survived by two children, although she had borne three. Just before her death, Brown had begun to attend Quaker services with her. Brown took her death as a wake-up call to more forcefully pursue a humanitarian agenda.

He explained to a friend, "I saw my slaves with my spiritual eyes as plainly as I see thee now, and it was given me as clearly to understand that the sacrifice that was called for of my hand was to give them their liberty."

So it was on November 10, 1773, that Moses Brown signed a deed freeing all his slaves on terms advantageous to them. He resigned from all the Brown businesses, disgusted with their involvement in the slave trade, and it was said that Moses "from that day forward became the most powerful opponent of slavery in Rhode Island."

Brown was not satisfied merely to free his own slaves. In 1774 he converted from Baptist to Quaker, becoming a stalwart champion of the Quaker reform movement, especially with regards to opposing the slave trade in all forms, through abolition and other methods. This did not please Brown's brother John, who remained heavily involved with the slave trade, but Moses advocated Rhode Island's 1774 ban on further importation of slaves.

His work against slavery from then on only increased. Moses Brown fought to pass the gradual manumission act of 1784 and helped pass a statute in 1787 forbidding anyone to outfit slave voyages in Rhode Island ports. In 1789 he helped found the Providence Society for Abolishing the Slave Trade, to help enforce the anti–slave trade legislation that had already been passed.

Moses argued that the Constitution should be ratified because it would bring economic stability and thus allow for banning all slave trade after 1808.

Moses Brown's house at Wayland and Humboldt Avenues became a major stop on the Underground Railroad. Providence was on the route from New Bedford (where escaping slaves arrived by ship) to Fall River and then Rhode Island. But Moses didn't merely offer his house as a stop on the Underground Railroad. He also was known for giving financial assistance to those in need. Brown often sent money to a former servant, Peggy, paying for her education, preaching, and eventually burial costs. Moses Brown "persisted in his efforts to improve the condition of the colored people in the state."

Moses also taught his son Obadiah Moses to actively oppose slavery like his father. Obadiah sponsored free blacks to help them find employment, helped with their finances, backed them up in legal disputes, and helped educate them. Obadiah Moses also sought to free slaves kidnapped from coastal cities and held by southern slave traders in the Deep South.

But it was Moses Brown, and his moment of clarity in 1773, that helped turn the tide against slavery in Rhode Island.

IMPATIENT INDEPENDENCE

1776

Most Americans know that Independence Day falls on July 4, 1776. But for Rhode Islanders, Independence Day actually falls two months earlier, celebrating Rhode Island's own declaration of independence on May 4, 1776.

As enshrined in the official Rhode Island statute:

> *TITLE 25*
> *Holidays and Days of Special Observance*
>
> *CHAPTER 25-2*
> *Days of Special Observance*
>
> *SECTION 25-2-1*
>
> *§ 25-2-1 Rhode Island Independence Day.—The fourth day of May in each and every year is established, in this state, as a day for celebration of Rhode Island*

independence, being a just tribute to the memory of the members of our general assembly, who, on the fourth day of May, 1776, in the State House at Providence, passed an act renouncing allegiance of the colony to the British crown and by the provisions of that act declared Rhode Island sovereign and independent, the first official act of its kind by any of the thirteen (13) American colonies.

Rhode Island had always been a state for independence, ever since its founding in 1636 by the rebellious Roger Williams, who had been exiled from the Massachusetts Bay Colony for daring to have differing religious beliefs. But a century later, Rhode Island had grown to be independent not only spiritually speaking, but financially speaking as well.

By the eighteenth century, Rhode Island was a veritable merchant's hub for the triangle trade, wherein molasses from the West Indies would come to Rhode Island to be distilled down into rum, and then the rum would be traded on the West African coast for slaves. The slaves in turn would endure a harsh voyage across the infamous "middle passage" through the Atlantic, to the Caribbean islands, where they would be sold to the West Indian plantation owners in exchange for a hefty cargo of molasses.

While the morality of the triangle trade may have been suspect, the profit was not; Rhode Island was becoming wealthy. Add to this that Rhode Islanders (rebellious by nature) had been smuggling for years, ignoring Britain's navigation acts, and generally creating a lucrative mercantile environment where Rhode Island was doing very well by the 1760s.

Naturally Britain wanted a bigger piece. So in 1764, when Britain began to crack down on colonial commerce with the Sugar Act (creating more control over trade, plus levying a hefty duty on the profitable molasses), Rhode Island was not about to give up its self-rule. Four years later in 1768, John Hancock's sloop *Liberty* was confiscated for smuggling. It was refitted as a British Royal Navy ship and used to patrol Rhode Island for customs violations. Within a year Newport's colonists burned the HMS *Liberty* in the first open act of rebellion against the British Crown. In 1772 the British tax schooner the HMS *Gaspee* ran aground, where it was also burned by angry Rhode Island colonists (as detailed elsewhere in this book).

The year 1774 brought Britain's "Intolerable Acts" (aka Coercive Acts), which between closing ports, forced quartering of soldiers, and taking over local government were sufficiently intolerable to foment revolution in full. The Providence Town Meeting was the first official government assembly to call for a general colonial congress to stand against Britain, and would later become the Continental Congress.

Tensions were high by 1775, when Providence supporters of the Boston Tea Party threw their own tea party at the Market House in February. In April the colonial legislature authorized a 1,500-man army of "observation," led by Nathanael Greene. And not much more than a year later, on May 4, 1776, Rhode Island became the first colony to declare independence from the British Crown—a full two months before everyone else.

The Rhode Island Historical Society still owns the actual document from that time that revokes Rhode Island's allegiance to King George III. It bears the header:

> *An Act Repealing an Act Intituled [sic], 'An Act for the More Effectual Securing to His Majesty the Allegiance of His Subjects in this His Colony and Dominion of Rhode-Island and Providence Plantations;' and Altering the Form of Commissions, of All Writs and Processes in the Courts, and of the Oaths Prescribed by Law.*

Printed by John Carter of Providence, this document was created on May 4, 1776, and officially declares independence for Rhode Island and Providence Plantations, as a fully legal act passed by the general assembly of Rhode Island. This was the first declaration of independence from England; the more famous Declaration of Independence from the united colonies-transforming-into-states would not come for two more months, on July 4.

Some have wondered at the fact that for all Rhode Island's patriotism, it was the last of the original colonies by far to join the Union and ratify the new American Constitution, waiting over a decade, until 1790. But the reasons are quite simple to understand, for they are the same: Rhode Island enjoyed being independent from all authority, both British and federal. And while the state was the last to join the Union, it should never be forgotten when discussing America's Declaration of Independence that Rhode Island came first by a full two months.

PIRATES OF THE *PROVIDENCE*

1779

The year 1779 marked one of the greatest hauls of the entire Revolutionary War. A number of British cargo ships were successfully attacked and the prizes totaled more than one million dollars. This was all accomplished thanks to the fearsome men of the *Providence*.

Not just Providence. THE *Providence,* a famed ship with a famed captain. Abraham Whipple was a name well known to the earliest settlers in Rhode Island. Born in Providence in 1733, Whipple spent much of his youth at sea, making alliances with the Brown family (who held much influence at the time). Whipple became a privateer under the command of Esek Hopkins, where he used his nautical knowledge to help sail the seas and gather goods for the colonists.

Whipple was swiftly appointed captain of a merchantman sailing in the West Indian trade, where he would hone his seafaring skills. The decades Whipple spent navigating through the northern harbors gave him the experience he would later rely upon to become a powerful commander.

Some historians believe that under letters of marque, Whipple engaged in privateering during the war with France. Before there was an actual navy, American colonists had no recourse except to rely upon the best privateers they could find. Privateers—so named because they were equipped by private enterprise rather than a government—fought for the prizes they would capture from the enemy. The government did, however, offer letters of marque to legitimize these expeditions. In return, privateers tithed 10 percent of the booty from any successful voyage back to the government.

Whipple's skill was recognized after a few years among the privateers, and he was eventually given command of the *Gamecock*. As captain of the *Gamecock,* between 1759 and 1760 Whipple captured well over a score of French vessels. He also captured the heart of Sarah Hopkins, the niece of Esek Hopkins, and the two were married.

Whipple was a key figure in the burning of the *Gaspee,* an event detailed elsewhere in this book, which was to be the spark of the Revolutionary War. In June 1772 Whipple and John Brown led a band of Rhode Islanders down to Narragansett Bay to burn the English revenue schooner *Gaspee,* which had run aground while chasing the packet ship *Hannah.*

In 1775 John Brown and the colonial General Assembly decided to create a Rhode Island navy to protect Newport, the first American navy (as opposed to merely privateer ships) of the Revolution. By now Whipple had become well known, and so when John Brown chartered his sloop the *Katy* as part of the two-vessel navy along with the *Washington,* he gave command to his best captain available: Abraham Whipple.

Whipple wasted no time in living up to his reputation. He declared that he would clear the bay of tenders from the British frigate *Rose,* which was off Newport at the time. The first cannon shot fired at the British navy was when Whipple's *Katy* attacked the British sloop *Diana,* easily capturing it and towing it back to Providence. When the *Rose* came to investigate, the American colonists reclaimed some of Newport's captured merchant ships.

Constant harassment of the *Rose* continued, and brought Whipple to the notice of the *Rose's* captain, James Wallace, who famously wrote the following note to Whipple:

"You, Abraham Whipple, on the 10th of June, 1772, burned His Majesty's vessel the *Gaspee,* and I will hang you at the yard-arm.— James Wallace."

Whipple replied:

"To Sir James Wallace: Sir, always catch a man before you hang him.—Abraham Whipple."

Whipple's flagship, the *Katy,* was taken into the Continental navy and renamed the *Providence.* But this was not the *Providence* with which Whipple would make his most famous run. Command of the *Providence* was given to John Hazard, and eventually John Paul Jones. Meanwhile, in December 1775 Whipple was given a larger ship: the twenty-four-gun frigate *Columbus.*

By April 1776 Whipple had commanded the *Columbus* during the first Continental navy expedition: a cruise to the Bahamas to seize military supplies from the British encampment at Nassau. The expedition was successful. And Whipple continued to be successful, capturing a few more British prizes over the next two years.

But it was in 1778 that Whipple would finally receive another frigate named *Providence*—this one a larger twenty-eight-gun vessel that had been built swiftly but blockaded in the Providence River for more than a year. In April Whipple outran Britain's blockade of Narragansett Bay under cover of rain and night, on a mission to deliver dispatches to France.

Well, mostly outran. Whipple had been running as stealthily as possible, enforcing silence and darkness aboard the *Providence* to avoid detection. But when he realized he was within striking distance, Whipple was unable to resist an opportunity to attack an enemy broadside, and fired upon the British frigate HMS *Lark.* After a brief skirmish, Whipple managed to escape the other British pursuers, and continue on toward France. Whipple arrived safely in France, delivering dispatches in Brest, and procuring guns and supplies at Paimboeuf.

But the very next year Whipple would claim his greatest prize. The *Providence* sailed from Boston on June 18, the flagship of a fleet also containing the *Ranger* and the *Queen of France.* A month later the fleet was amid heavy fog off the banks of Newfoundland when the Americans heard ship bells. They suddenly realized that they had sailed into Britain's Jamaica fleet, which boasted more than 150 sails and 60 cargo vessels.

Whipple concealed his guns and ran up the British flag, masquerading as British vessels in the fog. This allowed Whipple's ships to stay with the enemy fleet for most of the day without triggering any sort of alarm. Whipple quietly sent boats out one by one to take possession of unsuspecting ships. Without firing a single shot, Abraham Whipple commanded the most successful attack of the entire Revolutionary War.

When all was done, Whipple and his men had managed to capture eleven prizes from the British convoy and then slip away under cover of night. The fact that numerous seven hundred–ton ships were captured without firing a single shot is a testament to the captaincy of Abraham Whipple.

Eight of the ships were brought safely back to Boston, and the (previously financially struggling) colonial war effort was revitalized. It was the richest haul of the revolution, and the cargoes were auctioned off for a total of more than one million dollars, a veritable fortune in those days.

Whipple's raid is considered the most financially successful mission of the entire war. He received a share of prize money, as well as a letter from the Continental Congress congratulating him on his successful mission and requesting that he prepare the *Providence* for another cruise.

Sadly, Whipple's later mission was less successful. After being sent to Charleston, South Carolina, to help defend the port against the British, the *Providence* was taken captive along with Commodore Whipple in 1780.

Still, his successful raid against the Jamaica fleet remains a high point of the Revolutionary War.

PAPER PANIC

1786

By making some simple rules about paper money being accepted as legal tender—the same types of rules our federal government has today—in 1786 Rhode Island's government incurred the wrath and contempt of some creditors within the state and almost everyone in other states, who began to refer to Rhode Island by the pejorative name "Rogues' Island."

For better or worse, it was not the first time Rhode Island had acquired that particular moniker. Some people had called the state "Rogues' Island" ever since the day of its founding, out of contempt for Roger Williams and his belief in religious freedom.

Although for Roger Williams Rhode Island was a haven from religious persecution and a bastion for the liberty of conscience, other people were less enamored of his break from the Massachusetts Bay Colony, calling Rhode Island unpleasant names, such as "The Licentious Republic" and "The Sewer of New England." And while Roger Williams would believe a divine hand had guided him to a place he dubbed Providence, his lack of virtue in the eyes of others led them to call his land "Rogues' Island."

But the name faded from use for some time. Nearly a century and a half later, in 1778, Rhode Island ratified the Articles of Confederation, which brought the colony together with the other states under one central government—albeit an admittedly fairly weak one. Given the independent and rebellious nature of Rhode Island, submitting to a strong central power was less appealing, and so it is no surprise that when movements toward a stronger centralized federal power began to take hold two years later, Rhode Island was not eager.

By 1785 a number of Revolutionary War veterans had returned home to their farms to find that they were mired in debt. Britain was placing high tariffs and taxes on everything the states were trying to sell to them, and since there was no United States as of yet, each state did its own negotiating with Britain, thereby losing any advantage through unilateral negotiations. Technically John Adams was the ambassador to Britain, but naturally every state had its own representatives. This, along with the mounting debt, began to be too much for most farmers.

The problem was growing worse. Farmers fell so far behind on their payments that their homes were being foreclosed. Others were being sent to jail, dragged off to debtors' prison for being unable to make good on their debts. Riots broke out in many states, but as usual Rhode Island would find its own way of doing things.

The debt-ridden farmers demanded relief and began urging the state government to issue a new paper currency that could be used to pay off the debts—essentially an agrarian bailout for the farmers. This was opposed by the creditors, who had no desire to see the creation of a fiat currency mandated by the government, when they would prefer to collect their debts in coin.

Grand debates broke out in 1785, with farmers advocating for newly printed paper money, but their opponents managed to maintain control of the legislature, and so debts remained payable only in gold. But the newspapers took up the cause of the suffering farmers, who had organized themselves into a veritable agrarian-debtor revolt. When the next election came around in the spring, public opinion had shifted sufficiently to elect representatives in the Country Party, who were much more sympathetic to the idea of creating a paper currency by fiat, rather than one backed by gold.

The state government finally gave in to the farmers' demands, and the Country Party, which was led by Scituate's William West and South Kingstown's Jonathan Hazard, agreed to issue paper money. This was little surprise; those who had stood in the way of the paper currency were mostly Federalists from Providence. The Country Party, conversely, was composed of anti-federalists from the rural areas of the state. (This meant that they were also not eager to send delegates to the Constitutional Convention.)

But the most immediate game-changing action the Country Party took upon gaining control in 1786 was to issue a new paper currency. Half a million dollars were issued in scrip, printed up specifically to be loaned to the indebted farmers in exchange for a mortgage on their real estate. To make sure the new money had value, farmers couldn't get any of the scrip without signing a mortgage for twice the amount. The hope was that this would guarantee the new currency was as solid as gold, and in turn the farmers could use the currency to pay off their debts.

Unfortunately, the new currency began to depreciate almost instantly. When the farmers went to the store to buy basic dry goods and other necessities, they quickly found that the prices were rising. The farmers were unpleasantly surprised and believed that the merchants were conspiring against them by refusing to take their paper money at face value, and thwarting the government that had created this legal tender. (The creditors and merchants, for their part, had no desire to accept at face value a currency that was clearly dropping in value.)

To support its paper money, the Rhode Island legislature passed another law in that same year of 1786, known as the "forcing act." This law forced all creditors and merchants to accept the government scrip for its printed value in gold, under penalty of a hundred-dollar fine, with repeat offenders under threat of a five hundred–dollar fine, loss of voting rights, or even being sent to prison.

Shockingly, this did not inspire confidence in the new currency. The merchants in the cities simply closed up shop, rather than be forced to accept a worthless currency. It was at this time that residents of other states began referring to Rhode Island as "Rogue Island" or "Rogues' Island." The merchants refused to sell their goods. The frustrated farmers in turn decided not to send any produce into the cities where the merchants lived until shops were reopened. But by then the word of "Rogues' Island" had spread, and they found it difficult to sell their goods to other states.

One of the clauses of the forcing act stated that if any debtor should come across a merchant or creditor who refused to take paper money at face value, the debtor could simply bring the money to court and deposit it with the judge, who would issue a certificate officially discharging the debt. Boycotts arose in other states, telling everyone not to buy goods from "Rogues' Island," because it would help prop up the "rag-money" that was being forced upon people.

The case was finally brought to court when a Newport cabinet maker named Trevett attempted to purchase a joint of meat from a meat market run by a butcher named Weeden. Trevett offered the paper currency as payment, and Weeden refused to accept it at face value. Trevett brought the case before the court—an action he was eager to take, given that in such cases half of the fine for not accepting paper currency was paid to the plaintiff if successful.

The court case was tried in September, when crowds massed around the courthouse to cheer for their preferred side as if it were a prizefight. In a way, it was. After some consideration, the judges of Rhode Island's Supreme Court declared the forcing act unconstitutional. The initial charter of Rhode Island granted from England guaranteed certain property rights that were violated by the forcing acts, and therefore the inflation laws were declared to be in the wrong.

The legislature was not pleased, and convened a special session where they removed four of the judges responsible for overturning the act. In a bid to permanently install the paper money, the legislature attempted to enact a paper-money-accepting litmus test for all future holders of office, as well as a new and more vicious forcing act. But whether due to the boycotts, the rotting unsold farm goods, the departing merchant class, or just common sense, support for the forcing acts and paper money had finally dissipated. The new act failed to pass and the old act was repealed. And without any governmental force to artificially prop up the paper money's value, the paper dollar issued in May was worth roughly sixteen cents by November.

Rhode Island's paper money still stuck around until the state finally signed the Constitution, four years later, and a national currency was installed.

THE FIRST US SUPREME COURT DECISION

1791

It was 1775, and farmer William West was not having a good year.

"Farmer" may actually be the wrong word for William West of Scituate, Rhode Island. Sure, technically it described his occupation, as he had been a farmer for some time. It was said of William West that "it was not unusual for him to take 1,000 to 1,500 pounds of cheese to Providence at one time." But in addition to his farm work, West had served as deputy governor, was elected a dozen times as town representative, had served as a Rhode Island Supreme Court justice, and had even been a Revolutionary War general.

But despite all these challenging positions, farming is what caused him the most trouble. In 1763, after investing in a failed molasses sale, West was forced to take out a mortgage on his farm. And in 1775 the mortgage caught up with him, and West finally had difficulty paying the mortgage.

In honor of his long history of public service, the General Assembly allowed West to conduct a lottery for some of his real estate, to raise funds to pay off the mortgage. Conduct a lottery he did, and West was successful in divesting himself of some land in exchange for a small pile of currency.

The currency, in fact, was of particular value to West. The Rhode Island paper currency was one of the platform planks in West's Country Party, a political party opposing the ratification of the Constitution because, among other reasons, they were worried that adopting the Constitution would result in Rhode Island's paper currency no longer being accepted as legal tender.

These worries, in fact, were well founded. The holders of West's mortgage—the Jenckes family—refused to accept the Rhode Island paper currency and demanded payment in gold or silver. West pointed out that a Rhode Island law at the time specifically required that all creditors accept the state's paper currency as legal tender.

But the Jenckes family would hear none of it. They decided to sue West in Rhode Island's federal circuit court. They were represented by the husband of one of the Jenckes sisters, a man named David Barnes. Barnes was a clever attorney and argued that because he and his wife were residents of Massachusetts instead of Rhode Island, there was "diversity jurisdiction," which meant he shouldn't be beholden to Rhode Island state laws.

In June 1791 Barnes and West brought their case in front of Rhode Island's federal circuit court. The chief justice at the time was John Jay, who later would become the first chief justice of the US Supreme Court. West represented himself. Unfortunately, despite having served as a justice, West did not have any training as a lawyer. As a result, he lost his case.

West appealed the case to the US Supreme Court in Philadelphia. Since West couldn't get himself there, he hired Pennsylvania Attorney General William Bradford Jr. to represent him on appeal. (Unlike

West, Barnes made the long trip to Philly and was administered to the US Supreme Court bar on the morning of the argument.)

On August 2, 1791, the court heard *West v. Barnes,* the first case to be appealed and decided by the Supreme Court. Although the Supreme Court had existed for a few years, it had done little aside from swear in new attorneys. The Supreme Court had never heard an actual case until the *West* decision.

Barnes argued that West had not obtained a proper "writ of error," which was required by law to be certified by the US Supreme Court within ten days (thanks to the 1789 Judiciary Act). To be fair, obtaining a certification by the court in Philadelphia within ten days would have been very difficult, not to mention pricey, for poor Mr. West, especially given the eighteenth-century modes of travel from Providence. So, instead of having the US Supreme Court certify the writ, he simply had the local Rhode Island federal circuit court certify the writ.

Still, Barnes was not satisfied. Barnes argued that West had neglected a necessary statutory formality, and therefore his writ should be dismissed because a lower court could not certify a writ of error to itself. In response, Bradford argued that denying West (and other non-local citizens) the right to appeal because they lived so far away from Philly that they were outside a ten-day radius, was unjust.

Alas for Mr. West, the court agreed with Barnes, refusing to reinterpret the statute otherwise, and refusing to hear the rest of the case on the actual merits of the case itself. Each of the five sitting justices reluctantly issued an opinion in favor of Barnes, even though all of them seemed to sympathize with the unfortunate situation West was in.

Still, they wrote in their decision that only Congress could alter the meaning of a law. Regardless of whether they felt the current law was fair, the Supreme Court's job was to interpret the law, and the law as currently written was clearly in favor of Mr. Barnes.

Justice James Iredell's opinion shows him as very sympathetic to faraway citizens such as West who had trouble making the trip to Philly within the ten-day period. Iredell, to no avail, had looked through various bits of American and British common law, searching treatises by Sir Edward Coke and William Blackstone, in attempts to find any examples of lower courts issuing writs to themselves.

After the decision, Iredell wrote a letter to President George Washington, begging him to change the law. By 1792 the certification law was modified to allow faraway litigants to certify their writs in the local circuit courts.

Alas, it was too late for William West. He became the first person to lose a case in the US Supreme Court, and eventually lost his Scituate farm as well, selling it to his sons-in-law and (it is believed) using the proceeds to finally pay off that mortgage. After losing his farm, General West spent time in debtors' prison and died in poverty in 1816.

David Barnes, conversely, eventually became Rhode Island's US attorney and US District Court judge.

INDUSTRIAL REVOLUTION

1793

When Samuel Slater finally built his mill along the Blackstone River in 1793, it marked the beginning of the Industrial Revolution not only for Pawtucket, or Rhode Island, but also for the entire country. But the father of American industry did not come to build this mill by chance or indeed even arrive in Rhode Island unexpectedly.

Samuel Slater was born in Belper, Derbyshire, England, on June 9, 1768, the fifth of eight children. His father was a successful yeoman farmer and landowner, and although the Slaters were a family of farmers, at the young age of ten Samuel Slater began working at a local cotton mill for a man named Jedediah Strutt. Strutt was a partner of the famed British inventor Sir Richard Arkwright, who invented the spinning frame, also known as the water frame.

When Slater's father died in 1782, young Samuel Slater became apprenticed to Mr. Strutt. Although only fourteen years old at the time, Slater had an insatiable thirst for knowledge of the cotton manufacturing industry. Within eight years Slater had worked his way up through various roles until he finally became the superintendent of Strutt's entire mill.

In this more supervisory capacity, he learned about various aspects of the cotton manufacturing industry, such as organization and the practice of spinning, but specifically Slater managed to acquire a very thorough knowledge of the Arkwright spinning frames, and precisely how they worked.

This knowledge, it turned out, was highly in demand. Benjamin Franklin was an inventor of no mean skill, and led the Pennsylvania Society for the Encouragement of Manufactures and Useful Arts. They were offering good money for any inventions that might help improve the textile industry in America, since they were aware of Britain's advances in that area.

Britain, in turn, was aware that America was aware of this technological superiority, and so there was a law against the emigration of textile workers, or the export of any textile machinery, blueprints for textile machinery, and so on. Still, Slater felt he had already risen as high as he could within Britain's system and wanted to set off to make his fortune in America.

So it was in 1789 that Slater departed from England. He memorized everything he could about the details of the Arkwright machines, disguised himself as a farmer to elude the authorities, and then secretly emigrated to America—specifically to New York. He was not the first textile manufacturer to do so, but Slater's knowledge of the construction as well as the operation of textile machines put him a cut above his predecessors.

Still, when he arrived in New York, the job he took up at the local textile mill did not afford him the opportunities he had hoped for. They used antiquated spinning jennies, and Slater's vast knowledge of the Arkwright machines could not be brought to bear.

Meanwhile, that same year famed Rhode Island industrialist Moses Brown had just moved to Pawtucket. Moses Brown was attempting to start up his own textile mill venture, in a partnership with his cousin Smith Brown and his son-in-law William Almy. Brown had set up a mill with spinning jennies and had attempted to install a thirty-two-spindle frame based on Arkwright's designs that summer, but their mill was meeting with limited success.

And then their paths would cross. Slater had gotten word of Brown's venture, and particularly of his lack of success experimenting with his factory. He wrote a letter to Moses Brown:

> *Sir—A few days ago I was informed that you wanted a*
> *manager of cotton spinning, &c, in which business I flatter*
> *myself that I can give the greatest satisfaction, in making*
> *machinery, making good yarn, either for stockings or twist,*
> *as any that is made in England; as I have had opportunity,*
> *and an oversight, of Sir Richard Arkwright's works, and in*
> *Mr. Strutt's mill upwards of eight years . . . though I am*
> *in the New York manufactory . . . we have but one card,*
> *two machines, two spinning jennies, which I think are*
> *not worth using . . . my encouragement is pretty good, but*
> *should much rather have the care of the perpetual carding*
> *and spinning. My intention is to erect a perpetual card and*
> *spinning [referring to the Arkwright patents].*

Moses Brown eagerly replied, saying that he was seeking

> *the assistance of a person skilled in the frame or water*
> *spinning. An experiment has been made, which has*
> *failed, no person being acquainted with the business,*
> *and the frames imperfect. We are destitute of a person*
> *acquainted with water-frame spinning . . . if thou*
> *thought thou couldst perfect and conduct them to profit,*
> *if thou wilt come and do it, thou shalt have . . . the credit*

*as well as advantage of perfecting the first water-mill in
America, we should be glad to engage thy care so long as
they can be made profitable to both . . . if thou canst do
what thou sayest, I invite thee to come to Rhode Island.*

This was enough for Slater, who left New York to join Almy
& Brown in Providence. But when Slater arrived and looked at the
mill, he became downhearted and disappointed, claiming that the
current equipment was no good. The plan was hatched for Slater to
build a new series of machines based on the Arkwright patents he
had memorized. Slater demanded a craftsman to work under him,
one sworn to secrecy regarding the patterns and information required
to build such machines. But once the agreement was made, Slater
promised, "If I do not make as good yarn as they do in England, I
will have nothing for my services, but will throw the whole of what
I have attempted over the bridge."

Moses Brown offered Slater a partnership, along with William
Almy, Smith Brown, and Obadiah Brown. Slater would receive the
funds necessary to build the new water frames, as well as a half share
in profits. He was placed in charge of managing the new mill, and
set to work building the machines, doing much of the work himself, but also enlisting his bonded woodcutter and well-known local
craftsmen, such as wheelwright Sylvanus Brown, ironmaster Oziel
Wilkinson, and Leicester mechanic Pliny Earle.

What's more, Slater had no blueprints, and so was directing all of
this construction from memory. But he had a comprehensive knowledge of the Arkwright machines, and how they fit together into a continuous production system. In fact, Slater knew the machines so well,
he was able to adjust the designs on the fly to fit the needs of the local
factory. By the end of 1790, Slater had built carding, drawing, and rov-
ing machines, as well as a pair of seventy-two-spindled spinning frames.

In December 1790 the mill finally opened. At that time a team of nine children was hired to power the spindles with foot treadles, and another team of a dozen workers was hired to turn a giant treadmill for power. Thankfully, a waterwheel taken from an old mill was soon installed, replacing half of the need for human work with the glory of waterpower, so by 1791 Slater had some proper machinery in operation.

Finally, in 1793 Slater and Brown opened their first fully operational textile mill (the "Old Factory") in Pawtucket. It had the requisite machines, a waterwheel, waterway, dam, and of course, a giant mill. Here was the apotheosis of Slater's application of Richard Arkwright's designs. The Slater Mill had carding machines, drawing machines, and spinning machines, all operated by waterpower. This was the first such mill in America, and a spark for the Industrial Revolution.

Slater's insight was to perfect the one thing his factory could do best, and create a focused efficiency rather than trying to do all things related to cotton. Rather than spinning and weaving, as many other factories did, Samuel Slater focused solely on spinning, and on doing it better than anyone else. Likewise, rather than making goods to order, Slater maximized his efficiency by running his machines full tilt all the time, thereby lowering the marginal unit cost, which in turn raised the demand for his goods. His cotton yarn was sold primarily to weaving operations and other professionals who would focus on weaving it into cloth to sell, as well as housewives who simply wanted the cotton yarn for domestic use. But Slater had established himself as a dominating figure in this link of the cotton industry chain.

Slater Mill was the first truly successful factory in the entire country. But while the construction of Slater Mill in 1793 may have been the big bang that revolutionized American industry, Slater was far from finished. Five years later he built another mill, and then another one eight years after that. He hired children and families to work in his mill, starting Slater along a path that would eventually lead him to another great discovery: the company towns known as the "Rhode Island System." Slater would hire entire families at once, including the children, all to work in his mill. There was company-owned housing near the mills, and workers would shop at company stores and even attend company-owned churches and schools.

Slatersville was Samuel Slater's town, and this founder of the American Industrial Revolution would go on to own mills in many states, inspiring many copycats. But the first fully running successful factory, the one that kick-started American industry, was the first fully waterpowered factory that Samuel Slater completed in 1793.

ARCADE AT THE MALL

1828

While today's malls still occasionally contain an arcade, it used to be the other way around. Arcades were large lanes flanked by columns and pillars, covered by a roof, which had rows of shops on both sides. And in one such arcade was built America's oldest indoor shopping mall, back in 1828. Still standing today, the Providence Arcade is a testament to the construction of the times—and a tricky construction it was.

The year was 1827. At the time Providence was a prosperous seaport and a mercantile hub for the area. But Westminster Street was empty of shops. Back then the business section of town was on Water Street and North and South Main Streets. North Main was actually known as Cheapside back in the day, where merchants such as the firm of Watson & Gladding (which eventually became B. H. Gladding & Co.) had their shop at "the sign of the bunch of grapes." These shops served the small population of fourteen thousand who lived in Providence at the time.

Some have traced the popularity of arcades at the time back to the Madeleine of Napoleon in Paris. But from wherever they sprang, it cannot be denied that there were other examples of grand arcades going up at the same time. Arcades were being built in 1827 in places such as Stonington, Connecticut, New York City, and Philadelphia. Historians believe that the Providence arcade was inspired by the New York building. But the important fact is that the rest of these arcades have long since disappeared, while the Providence Arcade remains standing.

The birth of the Providence Arcade was a speculative venture, grown mainly from the mercantile mind of one Cyrus Butler. Butler, who oversaw the construction of the arcade, wanted to have shops west of the Providence River to present an alternative to Cheapside. The prosperous Brown family made most of the profits in that region, and Butler wanted a cut of the pie.

The arcade itself was a grand project—so grand, in fact, that it required not one but two architects to work on it. Russell Warren was one of the first generation of nineteenth-century architects, and like many of his peers was attempting to improve his lot from mere carpenter/designer into a full-fledged architect. Naturally, nothing could improve one's professional status more than designing Rhode Island's first commercial venture west of the Providence River.

The project was enormous. The building required a dozen massive granite columns, thirteen tons each and twenty feet tall. The granite came from the quarries in Johnston, which were the biggest in the country at the time. Legend has it that one of the columns, blasted out of Bear Rock ledge on the borders of Johnston, was completed by the workmen in only thirty days. Farmer James Olney hauled these giant stone pillars to Providence by team of oxen. He had to construct a special low gear for the carrying, and reinforce the bridge at Olneyville to bear the tremendous weight. But Olney managed to guide fifteen yoke of oxen through the woods to deliver their twelve-ton package.

The columns were the largest in the country at the time, and would remain among the largest for a century more. The building was an expression of grandiosity and the Greek revival, an impressive edifice on a monumental scale, the first work of this new style in Providence (as well as a first for Warren).

Russell Warren is generally credited with the northern facade on Westminster Street, an impressive display of hexa-style porticos supported by six massive columns of granite with smooth shafts and Ionic capitals, culminating in a pediment.

James Bucklin, who some historians argue was merely a consultant to Warren rather than a fully partnered designer trying to outdo Warren on the opposite entrance, is nonetheless generally credited with the southern entrance on Weybosset Street, which has a stepped parapet on top rather than a full pediment.

Regardless, when the Providence Arcade was finally completed in 1828, it was a sight to behold. Warren himself wrote about his masterpiece fifteen years later:

> Built of Granite Stone in 1827 and 1828, it fronts on two streets 74 feet on Westminster at the North and 74 feet on Weybosset at the South and is 216 feet in length it forms a transept or cross of a 194 feet by 42.
>
> The two fronts are ornamented with recess Porticos 15 feet deep each composed of six Grecin Ionic columns of 3 feet diameter and two square antaes and crowned with an Entabliture and cornice forming a Pediment. The whole hight of the front Colonade is 45 feet from the base to the Pediment.
>
> The Roof over the entrance hall or avenue is covered with glass 32 feet in width by 188 feet in length the roof over the stors is covered with tin. You enter the Portico by a flight of 4 steps running with the corner Buttments the entire length of the colonade.
>
> The hall or avenue running through from street to Street is 13 feet in width the building is three storys high there is 26 stors on each story making in all 78 stors.

> *The stors in the second and third storys you assend by*
> *two flights of stone steps under each Portico in each front.*
> *The Corridors forming the floors of the 2d and 3d*
> *storys are protected by a strong cast Iron ornimented bal-*
> *lustrade railing capt with Mahogany and running entire*
> *around the interior of the Building.*
> *The whole Cost Estimated at $145000.*

Indeed, $145,000 was a pretty penny even then, not to mention how many millions of dollars it would be worth in today's money. But Warren's description of dimensions and organization leaves out some important details of the construction of the Providence Arcade.

For example, the sidewalls were entirely unfurnished at the time, since other buildings were to go alongside them.

There is also the matter of initials carved into the column. Initially it was presumed that the "J.O. 1827" carved into a column was from James Olney. But newer theories suggest that Olney's son (who had the same initials), noticing a small defect in one of the columns, carved a plug out of Indian soapstone and marked it with his initials and the date when he wedged it into the column.

Regardless, the massive columns presented an impressive display that truly epitomized the Greek revival style of architecture, and when the Providence Arcade was completed in 1828, the country's oldest shopping mall was finally ready to run.

Sadly, despite being the first big commercial building west of the Providence River, and offering the convenience of many stores in one place, the Providence Arcade was not met with instant success. In fact, those who considered it too far from the Market Square in Providence's center of commerce referred to the arcade as "Butler's Folly," in mockery of Cyrus Butler, who had financed the construction. But the arcade, though not always met with commercial success, has truly withstood the test of time.

DORR TO FREEDOM

1842

It was an act of defiance on May 3, 1842, when the forces of Thomas Wilson Dorr held a grand inauguration for the new governor of Rhode Island. A great parade marched through the streets, filled with artisans, shopkeepers, mechanics, and even militia members. The only problem with this is that it was severely frowned upon by the other governor of Rhode Island, Samuel Ward King.

You might well ask, why were there two governors of Rhode Island? Well, the simple answer is that the winner of the election depends on which votes you count. The more complex answer may require a bit of background information.

Prior to the American Revolution, Rhode Island and Providence Plantations were still legally beholden to the Royal Charter of 1663, which laid out the operations of the state's governance. It detailed which branches of government held authority over the others, how representation was to be accounted by district, and who could vote. Specifically, it stated very clearly that the legislature held power over the judiciary, that delegates to Rhode Island's General Assembly would be assigned based on the population distribution recorded at the time of the charter (1663), and that ownership of a substantial amount of real estate was a requirement for voting and assembling in town meetings to conduct business and so forth.

Back in the 1600s, when the charter had been laid out, the landownership requirement did not seem onerous. After all, most of the colonists (the white male colonists, anyway) were farmers who had the required amount of land, and so this requirement for voting barely affected anyone. Fast forward nearly two centuries to the 1800s, and it was a different story. Thanks in part to the Industrial Revolution, urbanization, and population expansion, it was no longer the case that most colonists had the requisite $134 worth of land. In fact, by 1829 nearly two-thirds of Rhode Island's free white men did not possess enough land to vote.

The problem wasn't getting better. More and more people left the farms for the cities, and new immigrants came to work in the mills, further reducing the percentage of eligible voters. The seeds for a suffrage movement had already been planted, with various attempts to extend suffrage popping up over the past half century, ranging from Senator George Burrill's Fourth of July speech in 1797, to the 1821 referendum on a constitutional convention.

But in 1833 Providence carpenter Seth Luther wrote his "Address on the Right of Free Suffrage," claiming that political power in Rhode Island had become monopolized by "the mushroom lordlings, sprigs of nobility . . . small potato aristocrats." With the electorate now consisting of barely 40 percent of the state's white men, twelve thousand working Rhode Islanders were being forced to submit to five thousand landed gentry, all thanks to an ancient charter from a British monarch that many argued was a violation of the US Constitution.

Rhode Island, ever rebellious and independent, was one of the few states that had maintained a landowning qualification for voting.

But change was in the air, and the Rhode Island Suffrage Association was formed in 1840. A new pro-suffrage newspaper was created, called the *New Age*. Enter Thomas Wilson Dorr, a well-to-do lawyer very interested in extending the vote, who quickly became a leader in the suffrage movement.

On April 17, 1841, thousands marched through the streets of Providence in a parade demanding electoral reform, before meeting for a large dinner. In early May supporters of a wider suffrage held a meeting in Newport, where a resolution was passed stating that the people of Rhode Island had the right to create a constitution to combat the flaws in the current Royal Charter that were disenfranchising a majority of the populace.

This in turn spurred the General Assembly to call for a constitutional convention in late May. And in July the Suffrage Association made plans to hold its own constitutional convention. Thus two parallel constitutional conventions were going on at once. The suffrage group held meetings in late August where universal male suffrage determined the delegates who would attend the convention, which put together the "People's Constitution" by November. Meanwhile, the General Assembly sent its own delegates, chosen by the limited suffrage of the Royal Charter, to its own convention, which met in November.

Naturally, each group refused to recognize the primacy of the other group's rules. The result was two constitutions, one from the General Assembly still based on the British charter, and one from the Dorrite group based on universal white male suffrage. (Although Dorr and some others had initially wanted universal male suffrage, others insisted that the extension of suffrage remain only with whites.) A referendum on Dorr's constitution passed, although the General Assembly argued that since most of the votes were from non-landowners, that constitution was invalid.

Still, the people assembled for the Dorr constitution had stated, "We pledge ourselves, our substance and our sacred honors to stand by the People's Constitution, and firmly to maintain it, until overpowered by a superior force."

So it was that in April 1842, two simultaneous elections were held. Thomas Wilson Dorr was elected governor of the People's Party, in Providence. And Samuel Ward King was reelected governor of the conservative administration, in Newport. This could not persist. Samuel King got then-president John Tyler to promise the support of federal troops in case of an armed rebellion by Dorr's forces, since King had no plans to acknowledge their constitution.

All of which brings us back to May 3, 1842, the day when Governor Thomas Wilson Dorr was inaugurated, despite the fact that there was already a sitting governor of Rhode Island in the form of Samuel King. The Dorrite group met in Providence, and a great parade marched through the center of the city. Dorr's inauguration took place, and then the newly elected office holders were sworn in, after which the People's Legislature immediately convened and Dorr gave an inaugural address to the two houses of the (Dorrite) legislature.

Dorr's goals were clear. He wanted his new government to be the acknowledged government of the state. To this end, he implored that the new government take possession of all the artifacts of office in Rhode Island, including the state seal, the archives, and the state house itself. However, the People's Legislature was not eager to sanction the use of force and adjourned for two months. Still, Dorr wrote to President Tyler to ask for help in claiming what he felt was rightfully his.

Meanwhile, the General Assembly Legislature met in Newport, declared that insurrection was occurring in Rhode Island, and also asked President Tyler to dispatch federal troops to shut down the "lawless assemblages" that the People's Legislature was convening.

Tyler, for his part, took the prudent step of sending an observer and then deciding not to step into a situation that would clearly only be worsened by the presence of federal troops, saying, "The danger of domestic violence is hourly diminishing."

Dorr, however, was not to be dissuaded. The events of May 3 left him feeling a powerful governor supported by the will of the people, and it was this feeling that led him to launch an attack just over two weeks later upon the Cranston Street Arsenal, in Providence. He and his group of Dorrites marched on the state arsenal to demand its surrender. With him were many militiamen, such as Irish immigrants who supported Dorr since he had so recently granted them the vote.

But the Royal Charterites, who had taken to calling themselves the Law and Order Party (in opposition to Dorr's insurrection), defending the arsenal were not to be moved—included Dorr's own father, Sullivan Dorr. Governor King's militia defended the arsenal, Dorr's cannon misfired, and his assault on the arsenal was repelled. King issued a warrant for Dorr's arrest, which in turn caused Dorr to retreat to Chepachet. Charterite forces were sent to Woonsocket Village, which was so heavily fortified that the Dorr Rebellion mostly fell apart, and Dorr fled the state.

When Dorr returned to Rhode Island in 1843, he was put on trial for treason against the state (which is a bit odd since treason can technically be only against a country, but Rhode Island has always been a bizarre mix of city-state and nation-state), found guilty, and sentenced to solitary confinement in 1844.

POWDER BURNS AND SIDEBURNS

1853

In 1881 a man was buried in Rhode Island whose facial hair represented the Civil War. Although he was being laid into a grave as a man whose military career was not overly successful, his facial hair would live on forever bearing his name, even while his greatest achievement in firearms would be all but forgotten.

Ambrose Everett Burnside ("Amby," to his friends) was born on May 23, 1824, in a log cabin in Liberty, Indiana, without his trademark facial hair. The son of Edghill and Pamela Burnside, Ambrose had eight brothers and sisters. In his youth Burnside attended Liberty Seminary until his mother died in 1841, at which point his father apprenticed him as an indentured servant to a local merchant-tailor named John Dunham. Dunham was sufficiently impressed with Burnside's work ethic to help him set up his own tailor shop.

Young Ambrose Burnside had always shown an interest in the military, ranging from an intellectual interest in tactics to a boyish desire for adventure and excitement in the Wild West. Still, Ambrose's father was unconvinced he had the temperament for military service, despite his work ethic, because young Burnside was slow to anger.

Two incidents, however, changed his father's mind. First, a drunken customer one day entered Burnside's tailor shop, abusing the staff and customers. Ambrose hefted the man and threw him out the door, over a rail, and into the muddy street. This proved his ability to act when necessary. But the deciding factor was simply Burnside's interest in the military overall.

One day in the tailor shop Ambrose was explaining some standard military tactics to a friend, using buttons on the counter to represent soldiers, and manipulating them in accordance with military maneuvers. A congressman happened to enter the shop at that moment and remarked that Burnside should be in the military rather than in a tailor's shop. When the congressman began questioning the boy and realized Ambrose could quote from the US Army manual on military tactics, he more seriously suggested that Burnside enroll at West Point.

Burnside liked the idea, and so using his father's political connections, the young man enrolled at West Point in 1843. Considered the prankster of his group of friends, Burnside hung out with such future war heroes as Ulysses Grant at the academy. He was only an average student (foreshadowing the rest of his career) and graduated in 1847, choosing to join the artillery rather than the engineers for his first tour of duty.

Burnside was briefly commissioned as a brevet second lieutenant position in the Second Artillery, but by the time he arrived in Vera Cruz, hostilities were all but over, with the Mexican War winding down. Consequently, he served during the Mexican-American War mostly on garrison duty in Mexico City.

Once Burnside returned to America, he served under Captain Braxton Bragg with the Third US Artillery on the western frontier, a light artillery unit protecting western mail routes. In 1849, during a fight with the Apaches in New Mexico, an arrow struck Burnside in the neck, wounding him. Sadly, his well-known facial hair was only on the sides of his face, and not sufficiently concentrated around his neck to slow the arrow. However, he did eventually recover from the injury.

In 1852 Burnside was ordered to the East, assigned to the command of Fort Adams, in Newport, Rhode Island. It was here in Rhode Island, at a militia ball, that he would meet Mary Richmond Bishop, of Providence. The two would be married that same year, on April 27.

The following year, 1853, Ambrose Burnside would request permission from the secretary of war to have the Springfield Armory construct a model of a firearm of his own design. The reason was clear—to get a patent for the design of a rifle, the US Patent Office required the manufacturer to provide a working model, to go beyond proof of concept and show that there was actually something to patent.

As soon as Burnside had his working model in hand, he resigned his commission in the army (although he remained in the Rhode Island militia). Thus in 1853, Burnside left the army to establish the Burnside Arms Company—also known as Burnside & Bishop (named for his wife). It had to be admitted, Burnside sounded like a pretty good name for a gun company. But it may also have been an inauspicious one, as his company was destroyed by a fire the same year he founded it.

However, this was not to stop Burnside from continuing with the most important project of his career: designing a better breech-loading carbine. He took the insurance money and created the Bristol Firearms Company, which would continue to have as a flagship product the masterpiece of his own design, called the Burnside Breech Loader Carbine.

A great help to this goal was Massachusetts gunsmith George Foster, who not only helped Bristol Firearms to produce other gun parts to stay afloat while the carbine was perfected, but also helped perfect the carbine itself by suggesting gain-twist rifling. Unlike standard gun rifling, gain-twist rifling starts with slightly curved rifling, which grows to an increasing curve as the bullet moves down the barrel. The result is that the bullet's angular momentum slowly increases over the full length of the barrel, rather than going straight and acquiring spin only at the end.

The importance of this is that the torque is spread over a much longer section of the barrel, as opposed to concentrating all of it at one point. Because most previous guns failed to do this, the rifling at the point of highest torque would become eroded, and the gun would not work as well after repeated use.

This was not the only advantage of the Burnside carbine. The only other breech-loading weapon in use at the time was the Hall carbine. To put it mildly, the Hall carbine was not precision machinery. The Hall was known not only for leaking gas, but also for fouling and jamming, with cases often getting stuck in the breech block. Burnside used a tapered cartridge and a plunger on the back of the breech block, essentially making it adjustable for different cartridge lengths, while still maintaining a tight seal to prevent gas leakage. Burnside even manufactured his own cartridges, which used tallow and beeswax to prevent fouling.

Finally Burnside received his first patent on his original carbine on March 25, 1856. In 1857 the Burnside carbine won a competition at West Point against seventeen other carbine designs. It was clear that the Burnside carbine was a superior piece of machinery.

The secretary of war under President James Buchanan was a man by the name of John B. Floyd. Impressed with Burnside's rifle, Floyd signed a $100,000 contract to have Burnside equip the US Army with the weapon. Burnside, eager to supply his country's military, immediately began construction of new factories to meet the demand for arms, expanding the Bristol Firearms Company.

And then, a betrayal. As it turns out, Floyd had made a secret bargain with one of Burnside's competitors, who had bribed Floyd with the offer of a share of the profits from the lucrative military contract. Being the rascally sort, Floyd broke his contract with Burnside. Burnside, having poured all his money into new factories to produce weapons that now were no longer contracted, was almost broke.

Then Burnside ran for Congress in 1858 and lost, with the cost of the campaign making him even more broke. Then there was a fire at his factories, making Burnside completely broke. So broke, in fact, that he was forced to assign his beautiful carbine patent to his creditors.

Burnside's guns would go on to distinguish themselves in the Civil War. The Union cavalrymen ordered more than fifty-five thousand carbines of the Burnside variety, making it the third–most popular carbine of the entire Civil War. Not only did dozens of Union cavalry regiments arm themselves with the Burnside carbines, but many Confederates had captured the weapons and began arming themselves with Burnsides as well.

Alas, Burnside himself was not nearly so distinguished. As brigadier general of the Rhode Island militia, he raised a regiment: the First Rhode Island Volunteer Infantry. In 1861 he took command of the brigade at the first Battle of Bull Run. He led them in a moderately unsuccessful flank attack; nonetheless, he was later promoted.

Burnside was not a bad commander, but it would be hard to argue that he was a good one. He had his successful moments, such as an amphibious assault on Roanoke Island, which resulted in his promotion. In fact, he was even offered command of the Army of the Potomac, but realizing his relative military inexperience and lack of commanding skill, he declined the command.

After the second Battle of Bull Run, he was again offered command of the Army of the Potomac, and refused it again. After a poorly fought battle in Antietam, Burnside was once again offered command over the Army of the Potomac, and with this third request, rather than refusing, he finally acquiesced and accepted his assignment.

This turned out to be largely a mistake. As Burnside knew full well, he had advanced through the ranks through a combination of likeable character and name recognition from his carbine rifles. He had not advanced through the ranks due to military skill. He would go on to lead various ill-fated campaigns, culminating in a failed offensive against General Robert E. Lee in 1863 where Burnside's troops were so bogged down in winter rains that they were unable to advance at all. Known as the "Mud March," it was the end of Army Commander Burnside, who immediately tendered his resignation to President Abraham Lincoln.

Lincoln accepted the resignation from the post of commander but kept Burnside in the army. Alas, Burnside continued to not distinguish himself, whether through failing to send enough troops through the wilderness, or the fiasco during the Battle of the Crater, where he replaced his prepared regiment with one chosen at random at the last minute. Finally, in 1865 Burnside resigned from the army entirely.

The following year Burnside was elected governor of Rhode Island, a post he would hold for three more years. In 1871, when the National Rifle Association was started, Burnside was appointed its first president, no doubt based on the manufacture of his rifles rather than his dubious war record. He would be elected US Senator in 1874 and serve for the rest of his life.

Ambrose Burnside died of natural causes on September 13, 1881. He was buried in Providence's Swan Point Cemetery. He had been described as "a remarkably handsome man," but never as a great general. Few people know of Burnside's exploits in the Civil War, and most are even unaware of the Burnside carbine.

Thus the legacy of a man who devoted his life to the manufacture of a better carbine for Union soldiers has nothing to do with guns. No, Ambrose Burnside's legacy was his distinctive style of facial hair, which he wore throughout his life. His style of facial hair became popularized after his death and was named after him, which is why we now call that type of beard "sideburns."

A large equestrian statue of Burnside can be found in Kennedy Plaza in downtown Providence.

KING OF THE COURT

1881

America's first national tennis championship was held more than 130 years ago in Newport, Rhode Island, in 1881. Prior to that year, tennis around the country was a bit of a hodgepodge, as everyone had their own rules and exceptions. Thus, on May 21, 1881, the US National Lawn Tennis Association was officially formed, not only to codify a standard set of rules, but also to organize national competitions adhering to those new rules.

At the time Newport was the site of the US National Championship, which was played on grass courts. The championship moved to New York in 1915. It was renamed the US Open in 1968, and the courts were changed to clay in 1975. Even the US National Lawn Tennis Association dropped "National Lawn" from its name.

On August 31, 1881, the first US Tennis Championships were played. This historic match would later be called the US National Men's Singles Championship, but at the time only men were competing, so it was considered simply the championship. The Newport Casino hosted the tournament, which allowed only members of the US National Lawn Tennis Association (thus, Americans) to play.

The final match pitted Richard D. Sears against William E. Glyn.

Dick Sears was born in Boston on October 16, 1861, and was still a nineteen-year-old student at Harvard while competing in the inaugural US National Lawn Tennis Championships. He was not a fearsome-looking opponent, with a moustache and glasses, not to mention a necktie and cap that he wore on the court. But his aggressive play style of dashing into the forecourt to attack with swift volleys whenever possible was remarkably effective.

Bill Glyn was a member of the Staten Island Cricket and B.B. Club. Otherwise, he is well known only for losing to Dick Sears in straight sets in the championship match of 1881: 6–0, 6–3, 6–2.

To be fair to Glyn, it should be noted that Sears was an unparalleled tennis powerhouse. Not content with being the first nineteen-year-old to win in the United States, Sears won all—yes, all—of the US Tennis Championships for the next six years straight, not only in singles, but as half of the doubles championship teams as well. In fact, starting with his first victorious round of the inaugural championship in 1881, Sears went on an eighteen-match unbeaten streak that lasted through his victory in the 1887 championships (his seventh straight US Championship title). During his first three championships, Sears didn't even lose a single set.

Granted, Sears had one large advantage in subsequent years: Rules at the time dictated that the previous year's champion always got to defend his title. So all subsequent appearances by Sears were greatly aided by the fact that he didn't have to fight through the pack again. It all stemmed from his historic, unstoppable victory march during the very first US Tennis Championships in 1881.

Still, after being crowned the undisputed US champion in 1887, Richard Dudley Sears decided to retire undefeated from tennis. He then served for two years as the president of the US Tennis Association.

VAMPIRE CONSUMPTION

1892

Rhode Island's most famous vampire, Mercy Brown—possibly the last well-known vampire in the country—died on January 17, 1892. Mercy Lena Brown, at the young age of nineteen, had died from consumption, which today we call tuberculosis of the lungs. Regardless of what you call it, consumption was rampant at the time, and finally took Mercy Brown in 1892.

It was not, all things considered, a very good decade for her father, George T. Brown. George Brown was a farmer in the small rural town of Exeter. His troubles began in 1883, when his wife, Mary Eliza, died from consumption. The following year his older daughter, Mary Olive, would fall prey to the same disease, at twenty years old. His remaining two children, Mercy and her brother, Edwin, would also catch the disease a few years later.

The symptoms were all too common: a persistent cough, pallid color, a loss of weight and appetite, a feeling of pressure on the chest, general weakness. When Edwin and Mercy began to show signs of the disease, George Brown was devastated, having seen what it had done to his wife and older daughter.

Edwin moved away briefly, hoping that the clear waters of Colorado might halt his worsening condition, but alas, such did not seem to be the case. Edwin returned to Exeter in 1891. Mercy, meanwhile, contracted a more efficiently deadly variety of the "galloping" consumption and died on January 17, 1892.

In the winter, digging a grave through the frozen ground was exceedingly difficult, and so Mercy Brown was interred in the Chestnut Hill Cemetery Crypt. That, however, did not end her story.

Meanwhile, her surviving brother, Edwin, was growing worse by the month. He claimed that one night he felt Mercy sitting on his chest, trying to take his life away. Townsfolk starting reporting sightings of Mercy Brown walking about the cemetery. Mercy Brown, in the eyes of the town, was probably a vampire. And a dangerous vampire, who had returned from the grave to curse the rest of her family. And who knows, possibly the other townsfolk, too.

George, as the responsible father, had to do something. And in the 1890s the something they did was a little different. Medical science was not quite as advanced as it is today, and superstition reigned supreme. A folk remedy popular at the time was to exhume the body of a relative who had died from the disease, confirm that it was an accursed undead body, burn the heart, mix the ashes of the heart into a potion, and then drink them.

In other words, science.

Anyway, having lost two daughters and a wife, George Brown was desperate. It is unclear whether the idea came from George himself or from his neighbors who were afraid a vampiric curse would ruin the town, but for whatever reason, George Brown contacted Dr. Harold Metcalf of Wickford to join him and a posse of neighbors who trekked back into the cemetery on March 17, 1892.

There at the cemetery, the corpses of the recently deceased Brown family were exhumed for examination. George's wife, Mary Eliza, was nothing but a skeleton, and his older daughter, Mary Olive, was likewise mostly decayed, having been buried for some time. The body of Mercy Lena Brown, however, was not at all decayed. What's more, her corpse had shifted from its original position, and when the gathered townsfolk cut out her heart, it still dripped blood.

A modern explanation might be that the body was only recently dead and hadn't had any time to decay, especially with winter's chill preserving the organs inside. And indeed Dr. Metcalf suggested that the body's condition was perfectly within normal bounds. But the townsfolk took the strangeness of Mercy Brown's corpse as the final proof that she was indeed a vampire, and the cause of the tuberculosis plaguing the town.

So, the organs were drained of fluid, and Mercy Lena Brown's heart was burned to ashes on a nearby rock. The ashes, in turn, were mixed into a potion in keeping with the folkloric traditions, and given to young Edwin Brown to drink. As one might expect given the benefit of modern science, drinking the ashes of a corpse did not cure young Edwin, and indeed he died soon afterward, on May 2, 1892, of the same disease that had claimed his mother and siblings.

Some of the townsfolk, however, still argued that the cure had worked, because after Edwin's demise, nobody else in the town died from consumption that year.

Regardless, the *Providence Journal* printed an editorial at the time condemning the practice of exhuming bodies to burn their hearts as "barbaric," and this previously popular practice seems to have fallen out of favor since the passing of Mercy Brown.

Today Mercy Brown's gravestone can still be seen in the Chestnut Hill Cemetery, behind the Chestnut Hill Baptist Church, on Route 102, in Exeter.

RHODE ISLAND'S *TITANIC*

1907

It was a cold night on February 12, 1907, when the paddle-wheel steamer *Larchmont* was sailing toward New York. It had left port in Providence just the previous night, one of the "night boats" (evening-running ocean liners) of the Joy Line. But the night of February 12 brought a furious blizzard, with forty-five-knot winds and low visibility. The storm raged while the *Larchmont* passed through Block Island Sound toward New York City.

The *Larchmont* was roughly three miles from Watch Hill when suddenly Pilot Anson noticed two sets of lights off the bow. A gigantic 120-foot schooner, the *Harry P. Knowlton,* was loaded with coal and headed for Boston. Unfortunately, it was also being buffeted by the heavy winds and was on a collision course with the *Larchmont.* The steamer sounded the warning whistle and tried to veer out of the way of the oncoming coal schooner, but it was too late. The *Harry P. Knowlton* crashed into the front port side of the *Larchmont,* causing massive damage to the ship.

Moments later, explosions were heard from the boiler room. Any passengers not awakened by the initial crash were brought out of bed by the explosions, and as water rushed into the gaping holes in the steamer, it was clear that the *Larchmont* was going down.

The *Larchmont* itself was a side-wheel steamer originally constructed for the International Line in 1885, but was grounded in Boston Harbor after a collision left it abandoned. The Joy Line was a budget cruise line at the time, trying to compete along the routes between Providence, New York City, and Boston. While the Joy Line may have saved money by trying to restore an abandoned ship rather than building a new one, the *Larchmont* was beset by constant problems. In the half decade since 1902, the *Larchmont* had suffered two fires and a grounding before its final collision in 1907.

The *Larchmont* had departed Providence on the night of February 11, 1907, with an unknown number of passengers. The manifest sank with the *Larchmont* itself, and so there are only many conflicting estimates to go on. The Joy Line spokespeople put the figure at 120 passengers, newspapers used a higher estimate of 190 people, and the quartermaster would later claim that more than 350 people, between passengers and crew, were on the boat. However, a night boat on a stormy and cold February night was unlikely to draw large crowds, and so most modern estimates put the number of people at around 150 to 200.

Regardless, the *Larchmont* departed Providence with a cargo of freight and a strong northwest wind. It sailed right into the heart of the storm, and it was the next day, February 12, that the incident would occur. A warning was shouted, and a horn was blowing. The *Harry Knowlton,* captained by Frank P. Haley, was headed straight for the port side of the *Larchmont,* captained by George W. McVey. Nothing could be done; it was too late. The thunderous collision happened, with the *Harry Knowlton* striking hard into the *Larchmont* just in front of the port paddle box. The collision caused enough force to break through more than half of the width of the *Larchmont,* with the *Knowlton* penetrating nearly twenty feet.

The collision also damaged the *Larchmont's* engines and steam lines, quickly making further navigation impossible, and leaving the passengers trapped on a sinking vessel in the middle of a cold winter night. Within fifteen minutes, the *Larchmont* had completely sunk, stern first, into the briny deep. Or in this case, the aft deckhouse was torn off by the storm, and then the rest of the ship sank into the 140 feet of water three miles offshore.

The question remains as to who is to blame. As in most accident reports, each party was firmly convinced that the other party was at fault. Captain McVey of the *Larchmont* said that clearly the *Harry Knowlton* was at fault, because it didn't hold true to its initial course.

> *There was a schooner on the port and her crew seemed to have lost control of her. Without warning she luffed up and before we had an opportunity to do a thing headed for us. The quartermaster and pilot put the wheel hard aport, but the schooner was sailing along under a heavy breeze, and in a moment she had crashed into our port side, directly opposite the smokestack. I tried to signal to the engineer and mate, but the collision had broken the main steam pipe, filling that part of the boat with steam and cutting off communication with the pilot house.*

Conversely, Captain Frank Haley of the *Harry Knowlton* said that obviously the *Larchmont* was to blame for the disaster, since it refused to turn from its course to avoid the collision.

*A long time before the accident happened we had
sighted the* Larchmont *as she steamed steadily to the
westward. . . . Then we saw that the steamer seemed to
be heading directly for us. Some of us shouted a warning
and one member of the crew blew a horn constantly. I
scarcely knew what to do. I did not dare attempt to tack
to clear the part of the steamer, because I thought she
would turn out for us. When she was right ahead of us,
there was nothing for us to do but hit her.*

Regardless of who was at fault, it did not go well for those aboard the *Larchmont.* Passengers rushed to the decks, but many who arrived in a half-dressed state soon suffered from the freezing cold and icy waters. The cabins flooded, so going back for clothes was not an option. Everyone's extremities began to turn white with frost, and the passengers let out shrieks of pain as the icy waters rushed over their already shivering bodies.

The *Larchmont* quickly sank and barely had time to launch any boats. Captain McVey managed to escape on a boat with seven other crew members, and two lifeboats of passengers also made it ashore. A few passengers also survived in the deckhouse torn from the ship, which managed not to sink for a while longer.

Unfortunately, many of the passengers in the lifeboats and deck-house froze to death, along with (unsurprisingly) everyone who was in the water. Dozens of ice-encrusted bodies would wash ashore on Block Island following the disaster, the death toll from the freezing temperatures and icy waters reaching well over 140 people. In the end, only nine passengers survived, as well as ten crew members, including Captain McVey. And even they were in critical condition after the freezing cold.

The *Harry Knowlton,* however, was lucky enough to make it to shore.

LIKE STEALING FROM A BABE

1914

The year 1914 was when a young babe was demoted from the Boston Red Sox back to the Providence Grays. This babe was a mere nineteen years of age, and in that same year in the stadium at Rocky Point, said babe would be robbed of the first home run of his official career. In fact, he would make only one more home run during his entire minor league career. But this was not just any babe. This was The Babe: Babe Ruth.

Technically, ever since he was a babe, his name was George Herman Ruth. He spent most of his childhood in and out of St. Mary's Industrial School in Baltimore. This reform school to train delinquent orphans was a place Ruth attended, was released from in 1902, was sent back to in 1902, was released from again in 1902, was sent back to again in 1904, released once more in 1908, sent back to again, released from again, sent back to again, and finally released from in February 1914.

The final item on George Herman Ruth's official record at St. Mary's was a single sentence: "He is going to join the Balt. Baseball Team."

Young Ruth had played a lot of baseball at St. Mary's, partially because his instructor Brother Benedict was a huge baseball fan, but mainly because it was one of the only ways to keep Ruth out of trouble. (And young Ruth was trouble; he already had a tobacco habit at age seven!) Ruth excelled at all aspects of the national pastime, pitching, batting, and playing almost every position on the field with incredible skill.

Brother Benedict, suitably impressed, recommended George Herman Ruth to his friend Jack Dunn, who happened to own the Baltimore Orioles. Although Ruth was initially given a hard time, he was clearly a protégé of Jack Dunn and became known as "Jack's babe" or "one of Dunnie's babes." There were other babes at the time, but this babe, Babe Ruth, would become *The* Babe.

He would also quickly cease to be an Oriole; he was sold to the Boston Red Sox that summer for $2,900. At that time Babe Ruth was still playing as a pitcher. And thus after a short time with the Red Sox, Ruth had failed to impress. To be fair, it was a high standard to meet at the time; the Red Sox were fresh off of the 1912 world championship, and most of those championship players were still on the team. The competition for pitchers was fierce, including Ray Collins, Ernie Shore, Rube Foster, "Smokey" Joe Wood, and Dutch Leonard—the last two of whom won more than 75 percent of their games that year.

And the bench was fairly deep. Led by catcher "Rough" Bill Carrigan, the lineup consisted of Dick Hobitzell, Steve Yerkes, Everett Scott, Larry Gardner, Tris Speaker, Duffy Lewis, and Harry Hooper. Many of these men were considered to be some of the greatest players in all of baseball. Thus, even a player like Babe Ruth just didn't have a place on the team.

In August, after pitching for a combined total of only twenty-three innings, Ruth was sent back to the minor leagues, which meant playing for the Providence Grays in the International League.

Which brings us back to the home run that wasn't. George Herman "Babe" Ruth was pitching for the Providence Grays on a fine spring day. The stadium was Rocky Point Park, in Warwick, where the Grays had played many times before. But this time would be different—the very first time a young nineteen-year-old Babe Ruth would hit the ball out of the park in his professional career!

While at bat, Babe Ruth gave a mighty swing and hit the ball out of the field of play, right out of the baseball field and into the Narragansett Bay. The crowd cheered, and to the uneducated observer, it would look as though Babe Ruth had just scored his first home run.

However.

Rocky Point Park had a ground rule in those days, which was this: If you lose a ball into the water, then the ball is automatically scored as a ground rule triple. So while many people may recount the legend of having seen Babe Ruth hit his first home run at Rocky Point, the truth is slightly different. Spectators at the Rocky Point Park that day in 1914 saw Babe Ruth hit his first ball out of the park, but the box scores confirm that this out-of-the-park shot was recorded as only a triple.

Babe Ruth's first home run, and the only home run of his minor league career, would come months later during a September game in Toronto. But even with only a single home run, Babe Ruth's performance in 1914 helped lead the Providence Grays to the International League Championship. An 8–3 record as a pitcher helped lead Babe Ruth back to the Red Sox and eventually the Yankees, to become one of the greatest ballplayers of all time.

THE GIANT METAL TWINKIES THAT WON THE WAR

1941

The year was 1941. The world was in the midst of World War II. Denmark, Belgium, Norway, and France had just surrendered to Germany the previous year. Finally, in March, Congress had passed the Lend-Lease Act. This gave President Franklin Roosevelt the authority to lend, lease, transfer, or sell war goods to the government of any Allied country. More important, it signaled the end of American neutrality in World War II, and the reality that American troops would be sent overseas to be involved in combat.

The US Navy realized that they needed a cheap, lightweight, and portable shelter, one that was not only easy to transport, but easy to assemble without any machinery as well. Without a way to quickly house people and protect material at locations all over the world, they would be unable to fight the war.

Enter Quonset Point, an area in North Kingstown, Rhode Island, where a new naval base was just nearing completion. The George A. Fuller company was one of the two construction companies building the base, but with the Lend-Lease Act having finally been signed, the navy had a more important job for them. Peter Dejongh and Otto Brandenberger of the George A. Fuller company were asked to manufacture the new prefab huts for the navy—and to have units ready for deployment in no more than two months.

But what kind of structure would suffice? Traditional buildings took far too long to assemble and were too heavy. However, during the First World War, the British military had developed a structure called the Nissen hut. The Nissen hut was the first prefab building the world had seen, but the military felt that improvements could be made.

Dejongh and Brandenberger adapted the British design by using corrugated steel and semicircular steel arched ribs. The Anderson Sheet Metal Company, based in Providence, bent the corrugated steel sheets into the right shape. These could be attached with nuts and bolts, and the two ends were covered with a plywood facade, which had doors and windows built into it. The pressed wood of the fiberboard interior lining gave the new structure better stability than the Nissen hut, not to mention insulation, and a grooved plywood floor to make assembly even easier whether the building was placed on concrete, on pilings, or directly on the ground.

The original design was semicircular, sixteen feet wide by thirty-six feet long and framed with steel ribs that had an eight-foot radius. Covered with corrugated steel sheets on the sides, the huts of the first design were held up by heavy one-inch-thick T-shaped steel and angle iron arches, and were known among the men as a "T-rib" hut. A crew of eight men could assemble one in a single day.

A workable design had been achieved. The George A. Fuller Construction Company was quick to set up a production facility on Quonset Point, close to the recently constructed Davisville Naval Base. And there on Quonset Point, Captain Raymond V. Miller of the Civil Engineer Corps raised his concerns about what to call the new huts. If they called them Nissen huts, might the British claim patent infringement? Better to avoid the issue and have a new name. So, in honor of the location of their design and construction, they were named Quonset huts. (Quonset, incidentally, means "boundary" in the language of the Narragansett, the Native Americans who formerly lived in that area and gave it the name in the first place.)

With the Quonset hut now developed and named, it remained only to produce them as fast as humanly possible. Indeed, production had already started before the engineers were done working out all the kinks of the design. The advantage to this was that the first Quonset huts were produced within the two-month deadline, in May 1941, ready to be shipped overseas in bulk by June. These Quonset huts had plenty of open space inside and so could be flexibly pressed into use to serve any purpose, from barracks to bakeries, infirmaries to latrines.

However, there was a disadvantage to the speedy production, which was that the design had not yet been perfected. Although the first Quonset huts were shipped overseas in June 1941, there were concerns that the immediate curvature of the walls starting from the floor was an inefficient use of space, by reducing the effective width of the hut. A redesign included a vertical sidewall to make sure the interior had a width more reflective of the hut's footprint. In addition, the T-rib huts were difficult to crate and heavy to ship. Engineers developed a cheaper (and faster) way to assemble huts using welded steel strips called Stran-Steel, which were able to be assembled in a day by only six men, with no tools other than a hammer and nails.

In 1942 production of the original T-rib huts stopped entirely, and all subsequent huts were made with the redesigned Stran-Steel ribs. This marked not only the end of the T-rib hut, but also the end of the George A. Fuller factory on Quonset Point. Production of the newer huts was moved out to the Midwest, where such firms as the Great Lakes Steel Corporation would assemble them.

This is not to say that the Quonset huts were done evolving. Indeed, there was another redesign soon afterward, targeted at increasing the number of huts that could be shipped at once, by reducing both shipping space and weight. The newer redesign used even lighter, curved, corrugated, galvanized sheets as wall coverings. The newer hut was not only half a ton lighter than the previous models, but larger as well—twenty feet by forty-eight feet, as opposed to sixteen feet by thirty-six feet.

Another redesign eliminated the vertical "knee wall" on the sides of the huts, returning the corrugated walls to a design that curved upward from the floor. The new, larger huts did not lose as much space from the curvature as the previous huts. Yet another redesign combined flat corrugated siding with flat steel-framed windows. In 1943 the huts grew yet again, now a massive twenty feet by fifty-six feet, and four-foot overhangs were added to shield the hut from the elements (when being sent to regions where this would be a problem).

After all the redesigns, the Quonset hut required less shipping space than wood-framed tents to house the same number of men, and provided a much more reliable structure. More than 150,000 Quonset huts were manufactured during World War II. After the war many were sold off to the public as surplus by the military and are still standing today.

Granted, they may look like ridiculous giant metal Twinkies. But the Quonset hut was essential for the American war effort, and it can all be traced back to the hasty design and assembly of prototypes by the George A. Fuller Construction Company at Quonset Point, back in 1941.

JACK AND JACKIE GET MARRIED

1953

John Fitzgerald Kennedy was the son of Joe and Rose Kennedy. This was quite an advantage, since his mother was the daughter of Boston's former mayor, and his father was a former ambassador and multimillionaire. The result was that John—whom everyone called "Jack"—had everything he wanted growing up. Including eight brothers and sisters, with whom he was close.

In some ways he had to be; Jack's parents were often traveling abroad in Europe and elsewhere, so he had to rely on his siblings for support. But even more than that, Jack grew up reading many books. From spy novels, to historical novels, to poetry, Jack's interest in reading not only helped him get through childhood illness, but also led him to become very educated.

Naturally, the private schooling helped. Jack attended a succession of private schools from Riverdale Country School, to Canterbury School, to the Choate School, from which he would graduate in 1935 after being voted "Most Likely to Succeed."

After a brief enrollment at Princeton, from which he dropped out due to illness, Kennedy enrolled at Harvard University, where he graduated cum laude in 1940. He served in the navy during World War II and was awarded numerous medals.

But it was 1946 when Jack Kennedy would first join the US Congress as a representative from Massachusetts. Six years later, in 1952, he would unseat Henry Cabot Lodge Jr. for the Massachusetts Senate spot. And that same year, Jack was formally introduced to Jacqueline Bouvier at a dinner party thrown by mutual friends. (The two had met briefly a year prior, but only in passing.)

Jacqueline—Jackie, to her friends—was described as polished and elegant in her appearance. This was her usual modus operandi. Jack, meanwhile, was dressed in a disheveled suit, sports socks, and an old pair of trainers. But he was confident, funny, rich, and good-looking, and so the two quickly began dating.

Not that dating was easy. Jack was frequently unavailable, due to the hectic schedule of meetings and trips that accompanied his life and career. Nonetheless, Jackie called off her engagement to another young man and began spending more time with Jack, recognizing a kindred spirit and fellow intellectual and appreciator of historical novels.

Their engagement was officially announced on June 25, 1953. Less than three months later, on September 12, 1953, the two were married at St. Mary's Roman Catholic Church in Newport, Rhode Island. It was to be one of the biggest weddings ever, thanks to Joe Kennedy, who was stage managing the entire wedding to make sure the Kennedys remained as high-profile as possible.

More than 750 guests attended the ceremony at the picturesque St. Mary's, which had been decked out with pink gladioli and white chrysanthemums for the occasion. Archbishop Richard Cushing did the honors, marrying John Kennedy and Jacqueline Bouvier (Jack and Jackie, to their friends), after which Boston tenor Luigi Vena sang "Ave Maria."

The ceremony lasted forty minutes and included a papal blessing. Once the marriage was officially complete, the happy couple emerged into a crowd of thousands of well-wishers who cheered for the new marriage. The Kennedys then were escorted by motorcycle to Hammersmith Farm, the estate overlooking Narragansett Bay owned by Jacqueline's stepfather Hugh Auchincloss.

Here, more than twelve hundred guests were in attendance for the wedding reception, including most of the Washington elite. The receiving line took two full hours for the Kennedys to greet everyone. Finally the newly married couple were able to take the dance floor, as Meyer Davis and his orchestra played "I Married an Angel." The guests had champagne, and then the couple cut into an enormous five-tier wedding cake created by Plourde's Bakery in Fall River.

A luncheon of fruit cup, creamed chicken, and ice cream sculpted to resemble roses was served. It was a glorious day.

Later their marriage would become troubled, and Kennedy would become president and then get shot. But on that September day in 1953, everything seemed right with the world for Jack and Jackie.

BRINGING THEIR A-GAME

1964

The town of Johnston, Rhode Island, began cementing its reputation for political chicanery in 1964, thanks to the efforts of two gentlemen named Ralph (technically Raphael) Russo and Mario Russillo. At least that's what their names started as. The name changes to come would gain them national infamy in the political sphere.

In 1964 Councilman Ralph Russo decided to run for state senate as a Democrat. In the same year town clerk Mario Russillo (also a Democrat) decided to run for town administrator. Unfortunately for them, they were insurgent Democrats, and not officially endorsed candidates. And Rhode Island state law demanded that when it came to listing candidates on the ballots, endorsed candidates appeared in the first left-hand column, while unendorsed candidates (such as Russo and Russillo) were listed alphabetically from left to right.

Common wisdom held that people were more likely to vote for one of the first names they saw, not only because nobody wants to read through two dozen names for a race they don't care about, but also because it was slightly more difficult to pull voting machine levers for right-hand columns at the time. This was the reason for the rule, and it was also the reason that Russo and Russillo felt they needed a solution.

The two Democrats devised a scheme to work together to change their names before the election. Russillo, who was still serving as the town clerk, acted as a probate judge to sign official documents allowing Russo to change his last name to aRusso. And then Russillo's deputy took over as acting probate judge and signed official documents allowing Russillo to change his name to aRussillo.

Both petitions were witnessed by John P. Bourcier, another insurgent Democrat (and one who would eventually become a justice of the Rhode Island Supreme Court). The outflanked candidates were furious, and brought a case before the State Board of Elections, challenging the name changes in the courts. But Russo and Russillo—now aRusso and aRussillo—were victorious.

Thus, the 1964 elections had their names on the far left side of the ballot. aRusso did not manage to win his bid for a state senate seat, but aRussillo did claim victory and became Johnston's new town administrator. At this point he appointed aRusso as town finance director.

The name changes of 1964 were enough to bring the town of Johnston national derision, but the story doesn't end there. aRusso and aRussillo get even aRussillier. Four years later, aRusso and aRussillo were both competing for the town administrator position. aRussillo was the incumbent, and aRusso was his main competition. You might think that the little "a's" in front of their names would easily put them at the front of the ballot.

However, in the 1968 election, the Democratic machine had its own trick to play. They managed to find some people to forward as candidates who would come before aRussillo and aRusso alphabetically. So it was that the previously unknown candidates with the names of Acciardo, Anderson, and Arcand ended up on the ballot for the town administrator race. So many people were running that the ballot was more than three feet wide, once again putting aRussillo and aRusso in an unpleasant position.

Then aRussillo found out what was going on. Unwilling to be pushed to the far side of the ballot, he secretly went to a courtroom just before the filing deadline and had his name legally changed again—to aaRussillo. Thus, when the ballots finally appeared for the 1968 election of Johnston town administrator, aaRussillo was there on the left once again.

It is unclear whether this leftmost placement—or the resultant publicity—helped his campaign, but the fact of the matter is that aaRussillo won the election for town administrator by a mere thirty-nine votes, barely keeping his seat.

aaRussillo abdicated his post and declined to run again in 1970, leaving Ralph aRusso to win town administrator. The position eventually became mayor, and Ralph aRusso served as mayor of Johnston for twenty-four years. aaRussillo dropped the "a's" from his name in 1995 and returned to being simply Mario Russillo, but Mayor Ralph aRusso kept his for the rest of his life, and after he died in 1999, the state senate passed a resolution to officially express their sympathy to the aRusso family on the death of a beloved statesman.

Be that as it may, the wacky name-changing hijinks of aRusso and aaRussillo were the first time politicians had changed their names to be first on the ballot, and the events of 1964 ensured that Johnston would be mocked for many years to come.

THE TIMES WERE A-CHANGIN'
FOR FOLK

1965

When it comes to folk music, perhaps no artist is more beloved than the immortal Bob Dylan, who has been called the voice of a generation. However, on Sunday, July 25, 1965, he performed on a stage at the Newport Folk Festival, in an appearance that some have heralded as Dylan's turning point from folk music to rock music. One fact that can't be disputed is that here Dylan made his first live performance with an electric backup band, rather than just using his acoustic guitar.

It was not the first time Bob Dylan had performed at the Newport Folk Festival. That would be 1963, when a young twenty-two-year-old and not very well-known Bob Dylan appeared on stage as a guest of Joan Baez. But while Bob Dylan may have been mostly unknown when he walked onto the stage, everyone knew him by the end of that weekend. He won the crowd over, received standing ovations, and ended up the most popular performer of the festival, even among other folk legends, such as Pete Seeger, Joan Baez, and Peter, Paul, and Mary.

When Dylan returned to the festival the following year, the eager crowds were waiting.

Ronnie Gilbert of the Weavers introduced Bob Dylan and the audience went wild. Dylan was, once again, a smash success.

The year 1965 went a little differently.

Folk maven Alan Lomax was unimpressed with one of the bands performing at the festival that year, the Paul Butterfield Blues Band. Lomax said during a workshop at the festival, "Let's see if these Chicago boys know what the blues are all about." (Apparently they did, as their performance that year was well received by the crowd.) Dylan had performed on Saturday, July 24, and was irritated by Lomax's dismissal of the electric blues band, saying to himself, "Screw them if they think they can keep electricity out of here. I'll do it." Bob Dylan had suddenly decided he was going to play electric.

To be fair, the decision to play electric was only sudden insofar as it involved an electric performance at the folk festival. Apparently Dylan once slammed John Lennon and the Beatles by accusing their lyrics of vapidity: "You guys have nothing to say!" Lennon replied, "Well, you have no sound, man." This may well have left an impression on Dylan.

Dylan had already taken the bold step of putting some electric guitar on his January release of that year, *Bringing It All Back Home*. And it was little more than a month prior to the festival that Dylan had recorded "Like a Rolling Stone," which many consider his big shift from acoustic folk into electric rock. But the "Like a Rolling Stone" single had been released just days before the festival, so nobody expected electric music from Dylan.

And why would they? Dylan's decision was a last-minute response to Lomax's rudeness to the electric blues band. Dylan felt there was no reason electric instruments didn't belong on the stage with acoustic guitars, saying, "It's all music; no more, no less." Dylan found organist Al Kooper and said that he wanted to bring the "Rolling Stone" sound onto the stage. They recruited three members of the Butterfield band—Mike Bloomfield on guitar, Jerome Arnold on bass, and Sam Lay on the drums—as well as Barry Goldberg on piano. Dylan's secret impromptu band stole away on Saturday night to a Newport mansion being used by festival organizer George Wein, and they practiced until the break of dawn.

So it was on Sunday, July 25, 1965, Bob Dylan was getting ready to go on stage with an electric backup band that nobody expected. Not only the audience, but even the other performers did not expect it. Certainly the electric band would be a surprise to Pete Seeger, who announced that Sunday night's finale was "a message from today's folk musicians to a newborn baby about the world we live in." They had scheduled Dylan to go on just before the Georgia Sea Island Singers, and just after Cousin Emmy, both of which were very traditional folk bands.

Peter Yarrow, of Peter, Paul, and Mary, gave the introduction: "The person who's coming up now is a person who has in a sense changed the face of folk music to the large American public because he has brought to it a point of view of a poet. Ladies and gentlemen, the person that's going to come up now has a limited amount of time. . . . His name is Bob Dylan!"

Bob Dylan walked on stage in an orange shirt and black leather jacket, carrying an electric guitar. There was no time to do a sound check for his hastily assembled band, so they started right in playing "Maggie's Farm."

The audience went crazy, and not all in the good way. There were all sorts of sounds from the crowd, some cheering, and some booing, some jeering, and some yelling. The song finished to some applause, but other shouts of "Sell-out!" and "Judas!" and "Play folk music!" Dylan led the band into "Like a Rolling Stone," the song he'd just released as a single and wanted to try on stage, but again the audience response was a mix of cheering and hostility. The third song was "Phantom Engineer," but as the booing from the crowd increased, Dylan did not play a fourth song, and instead walked off with his band, leaving an empty stage and an awkward silence.

To this day it is unclear what caused all the yelling and booing. The prevailing theory is that the booing came from angry folk fans outraged by the fact that Bob Dylan was playing with an electric guitar. Others have said that the terrible sound quality from the audio technicians was the main reason for the crowd's booing, causing so much distortion in Dylan's voice that even Pete Seeger had said, "If I had an ax, I'd chop the microphone cable right now!" And still others argued that the booing was actually directed at Peter Yarrow, for limiting Dylan's spot to a mere fifteen minutes when most performers had gotten at least forty-five.

For whatever reason, and probably a mix of all three, a tremendous amount of yelling and booing occurred. Bob Dylan did not enjoy it, and left the stage. Peter Yarrow returned to the microphone and pleaded with Dylan to return to the stage. When Dylan agreed, Yarrow told the crowd that Dylan was getting his acoustic guitar. But as Dylan walked back on stage, now without electricity or a backup band, he realized he didn't have the right harmonica.

The crowd clamored for a Dylan classic, "Mr. Tambourine Man," and Dylan acquiesced, saying, "All right, I'll do that one for you." Dylan started strumming on his guitar, and then asked the audience "Does anybody have an E harmonica? An E harmonica, anybody, just throw them all up," and some were thrown on stage, as Dylan thanked the crowd. The acoustic rendition of "Mr. Tambourine Man" was Bob Dylan giving the crowd what they wanted, and it was greeted with strong applause (and no booing).

He did one more song, "It's All Over Now, Baby Blue," and the crowd went wild afterward, this time all screaming and clapping in approval. They called for more, but there was no more. For the crowd it was a victory; they again got Bob Dylan, folk legend, singing the songs for which they loved him best.

But for Bob Dylan, the night of July 25, 1965, was a disappointment. He was trying something new, trying something artistic by going electric, and was rebuffed by the crowd. The song they booed, "Like a Rolling Stone," would end up being named by *Rolling Stone* magazine as the greatest rock song of all time. But Dylan was hurt by the crowd's rejection of the new direction he wanted to take his music, and so after three straight years of performances, Bob Dylan did not return to the Newport Folk Festival for thirty-seven years.

When he finally appeared again in 2002, he was carrying his electric guitar and wearing a wig and a fake beard.

THE GREAT BLIZZARD

1978

February 6, 1978, *Providence Journal* weather page:

Heavy snow tonight, tapering off tomorrow

That Monday morning headline was, to put it mildly, a woeful underestimation. The first radio reports said there would be three to six inches. Snow fell at one to two inches per hour but did not stop. The next report predicted ten to twelve inches. But by the time the blizzard was over, it would set records for Rhode Island, at more than forty inches of snow in many parts of the state, and more than fifty inches in some parts of Cumberland.

The blizzard shut down the entire state for almost a week. Everyone of a certain age who grew up in Rhode Island can still remember the famed Blizzard of '78. Governor Don Carcieri remembered spending six hours trying to take Interstate 95 home during whiteout conditions, getting out to push his car every few feet.

But he had little choice. The storm hit just as Rhode Islanders were leaving work for the day. Hundreds of people were stranded in their cars on the highways and had to be rescued. Property damage ran to the millions of dollars. It didn't help that the snow continued for two days, and it was a particularly wet snow, leading not only to flooding but also to a number of downed trees and power lines. Roughly two dozen people were killed during the blizzard.

When the blizzard finally stopped, President Jimmy Carter declared Rhode Island (as well as both adjacent states) a federal disaster area. Driving was officially banned, and given a week when most people could not use their cars, and many were without power, it was almost like a return to simpler times.

For this reason, perhaps surprisingly, many Rhode Islanders have fond memories of the Blizzard of '78. Kids, certainly, had a never-before-seen abundance of snow to play with, whether making tunnels and snow forts or sledding in places that had never before been so completely covered in snow.

Adults, too, put on their skis and snowshoes to traverse the landscape. And even those who dug out and went on foot found it different than driving. People walked to the closest store to stock up on milk and bread, and everyone has stories.

David Porter, a snow plow driver, recalled the radio announcements on the day of the blizzard. "The storm set its teeth early. Noon came and went with me still doing electrical work for the rear lights. Not to worry, I had my trusty radio. . . . The NOAA [National Oceanic and Atmospheric Administration] guys continually reported on the storm. So many isobars, tracking such and such a path, total accumulation three to six inches. No problem, it must be almost over."

At 3 p.m. the report was still calling for three to six inches, but that's because the NOAA reports were updated only every three hours. In the meantime, more than six inches were already piled outside. Two hours later, NOAA was calling for ten to twelve inches, but from what Porter could see, a foot of snow had already fallen and it gave no sign of stopping. Later on the NOAA began using more vague accumulation estimates with phrases such as "two feet or more" and "in excess of."

By the time the worst of the blizzard was over, Porter said, "It was a constant battle to find places to push the huge piles of snow now obscuring the drives from the houses. We no longer cared about crowns and plant beds, we were operating in survival mode."

Personal Tales from Quahog.org

For those not working a plow during the storm, though, many treated it like a vacation. Beth, a student at Rhode Island School of Design at the time, explained that her twenty-minute foot commute took two hours that day. "There was so much snow that all you could see of the cars parked on the street were their antennas; everything else was completely buried. We built a snow house in the backyard that was two stories tall. I had a set of cross-country skis and explored the city. Took lots of pictures of I95 and 95 with all the stuck traffic. The payloaders the National Guard were using to clear out the city were big enough to comfortably fit ten people in them. On the Brown [University] campus, people built the most amazing snow sculptures. Since school was canceled and the city came to a standstill for two weeks, we stayed home and played lots of bridge, baked bread when our bread ran out, and generally had a good time with some friends."

Patti, who worked at Miriam Hospital, recalled being amazed when she woke up the day after the worst of the blizzard. "I couldn't get out of the apartment from the side-door entrance since the wall of a twenty-foot 'snowdrift' covered one side. The snow was at least waist high. It was incredible! I remember the camaraderie of neighbors and strangers. Cars and buses were covered in snow. Everything had stopped because the snow was overwhelming . . . yet it was beautiful. We helped one another, shared meals, shopped for elders, and made the best of it."

BASEBALL'S LONGEST GAME

1981

The longest game of professional baseball ever played took place at McCoy Stadium in Pawtucket, Rhode Island, on April 19, 1981. And April 20. And June 23. A total of eight and a half hours over three days, and thirty-three innings. But it started on April 19.

The Pawtucket Red Sox (Paw Sox) were hosting the Rochester Red Wings for a minor league AAA game at McCoy Stadium. After a slight delay due to lighting problems, the game started a few minutes past the scheduled time of 8 p.m. It went scoreless for six innings, and at the top of the seventh, the Red Wings scored a run.

There were no more runs until the bottom of the ninth, when Russ Laribee from the Paw Sox hit a sacrifice fly that drove in Chico Walker, tying the game at 1–1. So, with the score tied after nine innings, the game continued.

And continued. The game continued scoreless for inning after inning. Nine scoreless innings passed, an entire game's worth, and still the game continued. The players were tired, but the score was tied 1–1, and so they felt a duty to play on.

After two more scoreless innings, and then in the top of the twenty-first inning, Rochester scored a second run. Finally it looked as though the game would end.

Enter Wade Boggs. Boggs would go on to be a big star for the Boston Red Sox, but here on the farm team of the Paw Sox, he wasn't quite as famous. Still, he showed his stuff and got an RBI in the bottom of the twenty-first inning, allowing the Sox to score and tie the game once more.

Boggs recalled the reaction of his teammates: "A lot of people were saying, 'Yeah, yeah, we tied it, we tied it!' And then they said, 'Oh, no, what did you do? We could have gone home!' I didn't know if the guys on the team wanted to hug me or slug me."

Never has a baseball team been less excited to score a run. After all, it was already 1 a.m., but now the score was tied 2–2, and the game continued.

It shouldn't have. International League rules state that no inning in a minor league AAA game should start past 12:50 a.m. But due to a cruel twist of fate, the umpire's rulebook was missing this rule. The umpire, Denny Cregg, tried calling Harold Cooper, the president of the International League. Sadly, he couldn't get through, so the game continued.

In the twenty-second inning, Paw Sox manager Joe Morgan was ejected from the game by the umpire for arguing with the call of a foul ball. Morgan recalled returning to his office and overhearing the same thing from the clubhouses of both teams: "I don't care who, but somebody's got to score!"

Nobody did. Another nine scoreless innings went by, a whole other game's worth. The players had now played nonstop through the equivalent of more than three consecutive baseball games. When Rochester's relief pitcher told third baseman Cal Ripkin Jr. to watch for the bunt amid this third set of innings, Ripkin responded, "I've been watching for the bunt for twenty-three innings now!"

Two more scoreless innings went by. Finally the International League's president, Harold Cooper, picked up his phone. He was stunned to learn that the game was still going on that late into the morning. He demanded that the game be halted and postponed at the end of the current inning.

Doc Edwards, manager of the Red Wings, decided to take a gamble. When Tom Eaton lined a two-out base hit to right field in the top of the thirty-second, Edwards made the risky decision to wave John Hale home from second base. Edwards recalled, "As Hale rounded third, I could see that he was probably going to be out by thirty feet but I sent him anyway. It was wet out there, and I was hoping that the ball would slip out of [right fielder Sam Bowen's] hands and go into the stands."

But it was not to be. Bruce Hurst, Pawtucket's relief pitcher for the twenty-seventh through thirty-second innings, said, "I remember striking out Cal Ripken on a three-and-two breaking ball at four o'clock in the morning, and I don't think he ever forgave me."

The Paw Sox also failed to score in the bottom of the thirty-second inning. And so, at 4:07 a.m., after thirty-two innings and roughly eight hours of baseball, the game was finally postponed. Only nineteen fans had stayed up all night to watch the game, and these truly hard-core baseball fans were rewarded for their stamina with free season tickets from Pawtucket.

But the score was tied 2–2, so the game remained unfinished.

Two months later, on June 23, the Rochester Red Wings returned to Pawtucket to finish the game. This time the stands were packed. Thousands of people, including heavy coverage from national sports media, were present to see this historic event—a rarity, for minor league baseball.

It ended swiftly. The April portion of the game spanned more than eight hours over two days. But the June conclusion lasted only eighteen minutes, a single inning. In the bottom of the thirty-third inning, Paw Sox player Dave Koza was called to the plate with the bases loaded, and drove in the winning run.

"Having the bases loaded was a dream for me," said Koza. "I think anyone would have liked to have been in my shoes. Nothing I ever do in life will probably compare to this."

Baseball's longest game was finally over. Many of the players from that night went on to big-league fame, from Wade Boggs to Cal Ripkin Jr. And the night set all sorts of records—not only longest game, but also most at-bats, most strikeouts, most pitches thrown . . . literally a dozen professional records unlikely to be broken anytime soon.

The players may have gone on to the major leagues and more stardom, but nobody who participated in baseball's longest game will ever forget it.

RIVER RELOCATION

1984

There are two great historical examples of the moving of rivers by man. One was when Hercules was fabled to have single-handedly redirected the flow of an entire river. The other was the 1984 river relocation project that took place in Providence.

Prior to that time, the rivers had suffered decades of pollution from sewage and industrial waste—so much so, in fact, that the waters ran brown instead of blue. Eventually all hope of fixing the rivers was abandoned, and the whole thing was covered up with a giant parking lot. Well, technically since it was over a river, it was a bridge. In fact, the two acres of covered waterway made the Crawford Street Bridge the Guinness-approved world's widest at the time: a gigantic 1,147-foot parking deck with a well-nigh infinite expanse covering the polluted rivers.

But a world record didn't make up for the unpleasant reality: Covering up the murky waters had only created another eyesore with awful traffic patterns that caused many accidents. There needed to be a solution. Paving over yet more of the river to create additional concrete space was suggested, as the centerpiece of a plan developed in 1979 by the firm of Skidmore, Owens, and Merrill (SOM), which included various structural changes that would address the traffic issue somewhat.

However, the cost of the proposed solution was over $100 million, and since the rivers were already neglected and befouled, the plan to pave over yet more of them would do the rivers no favor. Ken Orenstein, then executive director of the Providence Foundation, was looking for alternative solutions, and thus William Warner, a Rhode Island architect, received a $100,000 grant in 1982 to study the possibility of restoring the rivers and making them part of the solution to the problem, rather than merely an obstacle to be paved over.

This was to be a turning point for Providence. While paving over things is certainly an American tradition, the possibility of a river revival in Providence became very appealing. The idea had some support from boosters such as James Rouse, who designed Boston's Quincy Market waterfront. Slide shows were made up to show the appealing possibilities of what a restored Providence might look like.

And indeed, the possibilities were appealing. November 1984 marked the official launch of the preliminary funding and approval for Phase 1 of Warner's project. Thanks largely to funding from the Providence Foundation, as well as some help from the National Endowment for the Arts, Warner could begin work on the three main goals of his initial development.

First, he had to relocate the famed World War Monument that stood in the center of the former roundabout. The roundabout was officially called Memorial Square, but locals always referred to it by the less complimentary name of Suicide Circle, thanks to the prodigious (and noisy) amount of traffic that was always flowing—however slowly—through the rotary. The World War Monument was partially dismantled and put into storage for a dozen years, finally returning to a location just a few hundred feet away in 1996.

Second, he had to realign the Woonasquatucket River to flow along its natural course. Warner's plan had all sorts of construction and demolition going on, with the Crawford Street Bridge being ripped up, new bridges being built, and roads being rerouted. But a post office stood downstream at the junction of the Woonasquatucket and Moshassuck Rivers, and could not be moved. Instead the rivers themselves were redirected. The confluence was essentially picked up and moved 150 yards east.

Third, and most ambitiously, he constructed a riverwalk and what would come to be known as Waterplace Park, in an attempt to bring the best of the Italian Renaissance into Providence. This part of the project was especially vast in scope: brand-new streets and cobblestone walkways, a cove enclosed by an open-air auditorium, Venetian-style bridges, pavilions, sculptures, fountains, and boat landings where gondolas would navigate the rivers just like in Italy.

Warner's ambitious river revival project, even in its first phase, was one of the largest urban renewal projects undertaken this century. Thankfully, the fact that few people actually lived in that area of downtown Providence made it easy for construction to occur without displacing any residents.

Later, of course, Waterplace Park would be augmented by the hundred blazing torches of *Waterfire*, a sculpture by Barnaby Evans that has inspired a recurring festival. But the turning point for Providence, the birth of its Renaissance, was the go-ahead given to William Warner in 1984 to begin his Herculean task.

DIVING DIPRETE

1998

It is probably safe to say that Rhode Island's politicians are not known for their honesty and upstanding virtue. But on December 29, 1998, Edward DiPrete became the first former governor in New England to be sentenced to prison, in this case for bribery, extortion, and racketeering.

DiPrete was Rhode Island's seventieth governor, serving from 1985 to 1991. As a Republican, DiPrete's three-term reign was considered highly unusual in Rhode Island, which had previously swung mostly Democratic in state elections. Born in Cranston, DiPrete graduated from the College of the Holy Cross and served as a lieutenant commander in the US Naval Reserves.

DiPrete's political career started in 1970, when he was elected to the Cranston School Committee. After being reelected in 1972, he served as chairman, before running for City Council in 1974, where he served for four years. In 1978 DiPrete became mayor of Cranston, a position he held until 1985, when he became governor of Rhode Island.

And it was during his six-year stint as governor, between 1985 and 1991, that Edward DiPrete allegedly carried out many illegal activities. The main thrust of most complaints against DiPrete was that he accepted bribes in exchange for favorable state contracts. Companies or individuals who wanted a contract with the state of Rhode Island under DiPrete's reign were expected to throw some money his way, whether as a political donor or otherwise.

This all came to light in 1994, when former governor DiPrete was indicted on criminal charges. Many accusations began to surface that implicated DiPrete in all manner of extortion and bribery associated with the handing out of lucrative state contracts. The entire political system seemed to be corrupt, with DiPrete leading a whole racketeering ring that included his son the engineer, two chief justices of the state Supreme Court, and even the mayor of Pawtucket. In short, DiPrete had created a "pay-to-play" environment for state contracts.

Perhaps the most comically embarrassing tale from DiPrete's reign as corrupt governor was his infamous "DiPrete Dumpster Dive." Apparently Edward DiPrete once received a ten thousand–dollar cash bribe at Walt's Roast Beef on Airport Road. But somehow he accidentally threw out the bribe with his sandwich wrapper! DiPrete was then caught jumping into the trash bin behind the restaurant to sift through the garbage in an attempt to retrieve his illegal bribe.

That $10,000 was not the biggest bribe DiPrete ever received—he admitted to illegally obtaining at least $250,000 in the racketeering through which he gave out state contracts, and some estimate that that number easily exceeds $300,000. But when most Rhode Islanders hear of Ed DiPrete, the Dumpster-diving episode is what comes to mind.

So, in 1994 former governor Edward DiPrete and his son, Dennis, were charged with twenty-four criminal counts, including perjury, bribery, extortion, and racketeering, in one of the biggest criminal cases in Rhode Island's history.

However.

It came to light that the prosecution had failed to provide evidence to the state that might be favorable to the accused governor. Defense attorney R. Robert Popeo had argued that the governor was innocent and that many of the state's charges were simply made up by untrustworthy witnesses who were trying to cut deals to avoid prosecution themselves. These deals had not been mentioned, so far, by the prosecution.

And several months into the trial, the prosecution finally turned over thirty boxes of files—files that contained information about deals that were made with some of the witnesses. These memos, previously undisclosed to the trial, showed that some of the witnesses had been offered inducements to testify.

So it was October 31, 1996, when prosecutor Michael Burns had to take the witness stand. He testified that although their star witness, Rodney Brusini, had been given immunity from perjury in exchange for his cooperation, Burns had no knowledge of this deal. Burns also denied that Brusini had been involved in his own bribery operation not under the realm of DiPrete.

However, one of the exhibits entered into evidence was a memo showing that Brusini had been taking two thousand dollars a month from a New York firm doing business with the state, thus proving that some of the shakedowns had been going on without DiPrete's knowledge. Under questioning from DiPrete's other defense lawyer, Richard Egbert, Burns revealed that he had read the memo back in 1993 but had "forgotten about it."

This was enough for judge Dominic Cresto, who ruled in 1997 that in withholding evidence, the prosecution had become guilty of prosecutorial misconduct. By failing to turn over all relevant documents and not divulging the immunity deals, they had compromised the fairness of the trial. And while the prosecution argued that the files had been lost in a vast sea of paperwork, the charges were thrown out.

However.

The Rhode Island Supreme Court met in January 1998 and reinstated the charges against the DiPretes. They ruled that Judge Cresto, even in the face of the delayed documents, had no right to dismiss a case entirely before the trial, and to exclude the testimony of the key witnesses. The DiPretes would be on trial after all. A new trial date was set for January 4, 1999.

But one month before the scheduled trial, in December 1998, Edward DiPrete surprised everyone by pleading guilty to no fewer than eighteen charges of corruption, including a number of felony charges, such as bribery, extortion, and racketeering. His son, Dennis, would not go to prison, and so in exchange for this leniency DiPrete agreed to the plea bargain and was sentenced to one year in a minimum-security prison.

It was the first time in Rhode Island, or even New England, that a governor was sent to prison. But despite the errors of the prosecution, it was finally clear that Edward DiPrete had accepted many bribes for contracts during his tenure as governor, and so in the last few days of 1998, the former governor was sentenced to a prison term for the following year.

BURNING THE HOUSE DOWN

2003

Thursday, February 20, 2003, was the date of one of the greatest nightclub tragedies in American history, which would eventually leave a hundred people dead and many more injured. At The Station, a nightclub in West Warwick on 211 Cowesett Avenue, the headlining band Great White was getting ready to begin their set.

Great White, in case you are not familiar, is the 1980s heavy metal group known for the hit song "Once Bitten, Twice Shy." It was just after 11 p.m., and everyone was excited for the show, with the audience pumping their fists in the air as the band took the stage.

Tour manager Dan Biechele set off the traditional pre-show pyrotechnics, a few cylinders at the back of the stage that sent a spray of sparks into the air. These pyrotechnics were gerbs, which are devices that produce a controlled spray of sparks. Biechele had set up the standard array of three gerbs to spray sparks for fifteen seconds, one pointing straight up and one on each side at a forty-five-degree angle. Each of these gerbs shot sparks roughly fifteen feet.

Unfortunately, some of the sparks from the sideways-angled pyrotechnics caught the sound insulation foam in the walls and ceilings surrounding the back of the stage near the drums. Normally this might not have been a problem, but this acoustic foam ignited because it was flammable.

There is some dispute as to who is primarily at fault for the flammable foam.

Later inquiries charged the nightclub owners, Michael and Jeffrey Derderian, with jail time for their role in purchasing and installing the flammable foam that led to the fire. Many other parties have been blamed for their involvement with the foam, from Sealed Air Corporation, which made the foam, to American Foam Corporation, which sold the foam to the nightclub.

But regardless of who was at fault, the fact remains that the foam ignited with alarming speed. It was less than six minutes from the first spark until the entire nightclub was engulfed in flames. The pyrotechnics shot off, and the band began playing their opening song, "Desert Moon," completely unaware of what was happening behind them.

The audience members who saw the fire initially presumed it was part of the act. But the flames spread from the walls to the ceiling, and smoke began to billow out of the foam, causing people to realize that this fire was not just part of the show.

Perhaps the man most ready to believe the fires were a danger was, oddly enough, a reporter who was filming the entire event. Brian Butler, of WPRI Channel 12, was on the scene doing a report on safety concerns at nightclubs. The previous month had seen a stampede that killed twenty-one people at a Chicago nightclub, and so he was filming live at The Station, talking about safety.

The result is that Butler had had his camera on the stage from the moment the first flame ignited. The entire horrifying event was recorded for the world to see. What Butler saw that night is a tragedy that millions have been able to watch unfold in real time.

The sparks begin setting fire to the acoustic foam high on a side wall at the back of the stage. One of the band members glanced backward and noticed the small fire but decided not to worry about it, and the band launched into "Desert Moon."

The flames spread to the ceiling, and then were on both sides of the stage. The crowd watched, entranced as the smoke built up, cheering for the band and possibly the fire as well. Roughly thirty seconds later, the fires had spread. The band stopped playing, and lead singer Jack Russell spoke into the microphone: "Wow, that's not good."

Some of the crowd was watching the fire and still rocking out. Others calmly began to make their way toward an exit—including Butler the news reporter, who backed his way out of the club. It was later estimated by Governor Donald Carcieri that any patrons who did not begin trying to flee within thirty seconds of the fire starting had little chance of survival.

The flames spread quickly, and within a minute, the entire stage was glowing white-hot and engulfed in flames. The band and their entourage fled for the west exit alongside the stage. A wall of speakers prevented most of the crowd from making it out the side exit, since the only other way to access that exit was blocked by a flaming stage.

Panic set in, as the fire grew to a raging inferno. Hundreds of people began to scramble for the exits. There was a crush at the main exit, as a pile of bodies and billowing thick smoke made it difficult to escape. Walls of fire made exiting through the doors almost impossible. Some patrons threw themselves through the windows to escape the blazing inferno. Five and a half minutes after the fire started, the entire building was ablaze.

Of the 462 people at the nightclub, 100 died, and 230 more were injured.

One of the first to escape, within the first minute, was the cameraman Brian Butler. He recalled the tragedy, watching the flames climb up the ceiling, as most of the crowd took a few seconds to realize what was happening: "At first, there was no panic. Everybody just kind of turned. Most people still just stood there." With most of the flame and smoke confined to the main room, many did not realize the terrible danger they were in.

Butler fled the building and then realized the back door was blocked. He recalled watching a bottleneck form at the front door. "You saw people stacked on top of each other, trying to get out of the front door." The video showed piles of people lying on top of each other, trying to push their way out of the club before burning alive.

Butler recalled how swiftly everything happened: "And by then the black smoke was pouring out over their heads. . . . I never expected it to take off as fast as it did. It just—it was so fast. It had to be two minutes tops before the whole place was black smoke."

Clubgoer Lisa Shea shuddered to recall her experience: "The whole place got tons of black smoke. We were breathing black smoke. I got knocked on the ground. People were standing on my back, my head. I was holding my head, and I said, 'I'm going to die here.' All I could think about was my mother, and I said, 'I got to get up. I got to get up.'"

Another survivor, Erin Pucino, said she owed her life to people who tried to help. "There were two girls standing at the railing, and they tried pulling me and they couldn't get me. Then there was a man standing in front of me, and he started pulling, and he got me out. He pulled me out of the pile."

By the time the fire alarms had gone off, everyone was in a panicked stampede through the narrow hallway leading to the front door. The resultant pileup led to many deaths and injuries among the patrons and staff, including burns, smoke inhalation, and trampling, and eventually the collapse of the entire building. Deaths during the incident included Great White's lead guitarist, Ty Longley.

First responders in fire and rescue crews may have saved as many as one hundred lives by pulling people out, according to Governor Carcieri. At least 187 injured people were taken to nearby hospitals, where 81 were admitted. Ten were flown to the nearest burn centers in Massachusetts.

It's hard to know who to blame for the fire. The club owners, Michael and Jeffrey Derderian, claimed not to know the band had pyrotechnics, but the band's tour manager, Dan Biechele, claimed to have set it up with the club. Regardless, Great White did not have the required city permit for a pyrotechnics display. And The Station did not have a sprinkler system, which could have prevented the entire tragedy.

Regardless, Thursday, February 20, 2003, will remain a tragedy etched in the minds of Rhode Islanders.

Biechele, Great White's former road manager, pled guilty to one hundred counts of involuntary manslaughter on February 7, 2006. He was sentenced to serve four years in prison with eleven more as a suspended sentence, plus three years probation, and was released on parole in March 2008.

Station nightclub owners Michael and Jeffrey Derderian pled "no contest" on September 21, 2006. Michael received the same sentence as Biechele, and was released on parole in June 2009. Jeffrey received a ten-year suspended sentence, three years probation, and five hundred hours of community service.

THE SURVIVOR GOES DOWN

2005

You may be familiar with Richard Hatch. Don't feel bad if you aren't; this likely only makes you smarter than those of us who are. But Richard Hatch was a Newport native who won the very first season of the CBS reality series *Survivor* in 2000.

Hatch was thirty-nine years old at the time, and working as a corporate trainer. Previously he had served in the US Army after attending the US Military Academy, and had also held various other jobs, including bartender, car salesman, and real estate agent.

No doubt, all of these provided skills that helped move Hatch toward victory. His bartending presumably gave him a background in talking to people. His car sales and real estate jobs presumably left him familiar with how best to negotiate deals. His army background gave him discipline. And during that first season of *Survivor*, Hatch himself mentioned that he felt his experience as a corporate trainer would give him an edge over the other contestants.

Also, he chose to be nude a lot (for reasons that are unclear), leading David Letterman to refer to him as "the fat naked guy." Regardless, he used his army background and quickly allied with a former navy SEAL, and their alliance led both of them to the final three. In the end it was Hatch who emerged victorious, and in addition to a modicum of celebrity, Hatch walked away with a million-dollar prize.

And this is where the story becomes interesting. In 2005 Hatch was charged with tax evasion. The reason? Apparently the million dollars he won for the season of *Survivor* (plus an additional ten thousand dollars the show paid him for a finale appearance) never appeared on Hatch's 2000 tax return. And $300,000 that he was paid by a Boston radio station was unmentioned on his 2001 return.

Normally when accused of inaccuracies with income tax reporting, you hire a lawyer and try to hide income or argue that you never made that much money. But this is harder to do when you've appeared on television and radio and large swaths of the country know exactly how much money you made, and how, when, and why.

Additionally, it's hard to get anyone to trust you—or for that matter, any jury to sympathize with you—when America has seen you spend a season manipulating people to win money. Prosecutors offered Hatch a deal where he could plead guilty to the two counts of tax evasion in exchange for a more lenient sentence than the ten-year maximum, but although Hatch initially found the deal appealing, he eventually backed out of it. He was indicted in 2005.

During his trial, Hatch's lawyer, Michael Minns, argued that Hatch caught fellow contestants cheating and had struck a secret deal with the show's producers to pay his taxes if he won. But Minns never asked Hatch to verify the existence of any such deal, or cheating, under oath. Hatch did testify that he believed the producers were going to pay his taxes, but the producers testified that the contract clearly spelled out that the tax burden would lie with Hatch.

Minns changed strategies and began referring to Hatch as the "world's worst bookkeeper," but to little avail. Hatch was found guilty of tax evasion, and in 2006 he was sentenced to fifty-one months in jail. In 2009 he was released to home confinement, where he gave a television interview claiming that the trial had been unfair.

"I know without question there were personal issues involved for the prosecutor," said Hatch, a gay man who also blamed the judge for not letting potential jurors first be questioned about their feelings toward gays.

Hatch went on to appear on the television show *Celebrity Apprentice,* but as of 2011 he had still never refiled his 2000 tax forms or paid the money he owes.

SOCK IT TO ME

2011

Rhode Island may be the smallest state, but in 2011 members of the Rhode Island Sewing Network and Project Undercover set out to make the world's biggest sock.

This sock was put together to call attention to the state's biggest sock problem: namely, that many children do not have underwear and socks because such items are not handed down or found at donation centers, and families in poverty cannot always afford to buy new clothes. This is the focus of Project Undercover, a charity run by executive director Abby McQuade.

McQuade estimates that more than forty thousand children from families below the poverty line live in Rhode Island, leaving nearly one in six of the state's children without underclothing. She started the project nearly two decades ago under the auspices of the Girl Scouts and Rhode Island Donation Exchange, and Project Undercover finally became a full-fledged charity in 2010.

Still, it hadn't been getting a lot of publicity. And that's when board member Jeanette St. Pierre hatched a brilliant idea: Why not make an attempt at a Guinness World Record to raise awareness of Project Undercover and its mission, to distribute nearly a quarter of a million items a year to families in need?

So it was that in September 2011, dozens of volunteers from the Rhode Island Sewing Network pitched in to sew and construct the world's largest sock. Various members of the sewing network brought their sewing machines, irons, and other equipment to the classroom space at Blaine's Sewing Machine Center, at 1280 Oaklawn Avenue in Cranston. Some of them had met in the University of Rhode Island's master seamstress program, and while many of them had been sewing for decades if not their entire lives, none of them had ever worked on a project of this magnitude.

The planned size of the finished sock: thirty-two feet high and seventeen feet wide. This would easily trump the previous world's biggest sock, a sixteen-foot-by-fourteen-foot Austrian sock put together in 2005. For Rhode Island to create the new sock, organizers estimated that it would take six hundred sewer-hours over three months, two hundred yards of fabric, and thirteen thousand yards of thread. Thankfully, the Rhode Island Sewing Network was on hand to donate skilled labor.

Volunteers for the project included Sue Wiersma, Rosemary Gomes, Phylis Montgomery, Susan Love, Sheila Vargas, Jean Sahakian, Anne McCann, Maureen Agnew, and dozens of other skilled sewers and coordinators. Ocean State Job Lot helped sponsor the event, while the Rhode Island Sewing Network volunteer brigade used their time and skill to set to work creating the world's biggest sock.

Putting together a sock of that size has to be done in stages, with planning. A scale model of the sock was sewn together, marked up to show the different sections. Even once the sections were all laid out, it took three teams of volunteers just to press the finished sections, and stack them up with notes pinned to each section detailing how and where it should be sewn during the final assembly process.

And finally, in December 2011, the sock was completed. And what's more, it was even larger than the initial estimated plans. The final sock was thirty-two feet seven inches, by twenty-two feet six inches, by eight feet two inches. And one gigantic foot is what it would take to fit inside. The enormous sock, which is cream and brown colored, was hung from the third-floor balcony of the Rhode Island Convention Center—although it did reach all the way down to the first floor.

Official Guinness World Records Adjudicator Danny Girton Jr. attended the unfurling at the Rhode Island Convention Center to verify the record-breaking nature of the new official world's biggest sock. Indeed, Abby McQuade and board president Richard Fleischer were awarded an official certificate from Guinness World Records proclaiming their sock's world record.

So, six hundred feet of cotton and forty-two thousand feet of cotton thread were sewn into the world's biggest sock, all to raise awareness of the big sock (and other undergarment) problem that Project Undercover hopes to combat. For more information, visit www.projectundercover.org.

RHODE ISLAND FACTS AND FIRSTS

FACTS

- Rhode Island and Providence Plantations is America's smallest state, with America's smallest state motto: "Hope."

- However, the State of Rhode Island and Providence Plantations has America's longest official state name. Its official nickname is "The Ocean State," although unofficially it is often called "Little Rhody."

- Rhode Island is divided into five counties, but there is no county government.

- Rhode Island has its own lexicon for things you eat or drink. "Cabinets" are milk shakes, "gaggers" or "bellybusters" are hot wieners, "grinders" are hoagies, "bubbler" is a water fountain. The aforementioned are pronounced "gaggahz," "bellybustahs," and "bubblah," because Rhode Islanders tend to remove the "r's" from the end of most words when pronouncing them, and place them all at the end of "idea."

- Rhode Island has more Dunkin' Donuts per square mile, and per capita, than any other state, despite the fact that the chain is based in Massachusetts.

- Rhode Island is the second–most densely populated state in the country, second only to New Jersey.

- Quahog, Rhode Island, the town immortalized in the *Family Guy* television show, is fictional. However, the quahog is a bivalve type of clam that is harvested and eaten in the state.

- The state bird is the Rhode Island Red, and the state mineral is cumberlandite, which is not found north of Cumberland.

- The state song, "Rhode Island, It's for Me," was written by a stand-up comedian named Charlie Hall, who used to lead a satirical group called the Ocean State Follies.

- Rhode Island is the costume jewelry capital of the world, an industry that began in Providence in 1794 when the Dodge Brothers developed the idea of gold plating.

- Rhode Island was the last of the thirteen original colonies to ratify the US Constitution, in 1790.

- Rhode Island was the only state not to ratify the Eighteenth Amendment, the prohibition amendment.

- Rhode Island is the only state that still recognizes V-J (Victory over Japan) Day as an official state holiday, called "Victory Day."

- The Rhode Island State House is the fourth-largest self-supporting marble dome in the world, and is topped by a statue of *The Independent Man,* in honor of the independence upon which the state was founded, and the stubborn independence it retains to this day.

- The state house is a giant marble building that looks very similar to the US Capitol.

- In spite of this, Rhode Island's most recognizable landmark is the "Big Blue Bug," a termite that sits atop the roof of Big Blue Bug Solutions in Providence. At fifty-eight feet long, it is the world's largest bug, and has appeared in numerous movies.

FIRSTS

- First Baptist church in America, founded in Providence by Roger Williams in 1638.

- First synagogue in America, Touro Synagogue in Newport in 1762, which has a letter from George Washington sent to the synagogue in 1790, and America's oldest Torah at five hundred years old.

- First street in the country to use gaslights: Pelham Street in Newport in 1806.

- First law prohibiting slavery in North America enacted in 1652, and first colony banning the importation of slaves in 1774.

- First July 4th parade still running today is held annually in Bristol, started 1785.

- First female newspaper editor in America, Ann Smith Franklin of the *Newport Mercury,* in 1762.

- First US strike that also included women, in Pawtucket, 1824.

- First lunch wagon in America, run by Walter Scott in Providence, 1872.

- First nine-hole golf course in America, in Newport in 1890. Newport was also the location of the first US Open, in 1895.

- First NFL night game was in 1929, at Providence's Kinsley Park.

- First American black army unit, the First Rhode Island Regiment, formed in 1778.

- First US polo game, played in Newport in 1876.

- First circus in the United States in Newport in 1774.

- First US state-owned airport in Warwick in 1931.

- First US self-service discount department store, Ann & Hope, in Cumberland, 1953.

- First US jazz festival, Newport, 1954.

- First torpedo boat, the *Stiletto,* was built in Bristol in 1887.

- First state to enforce mandatory recycling in 1986.

- First jail sentence for speeding in an automobile, assigned by Judge Darius Baker in Newport in 1904. The illegal speed was fifteen miles per hour.

- First state to require driver's licenses, 1908.

- First US manufactured baby carriages, Westerly, 1841.

- First basketball hoop with netting created in Providence, 1893.

BIBLIOGRAPHY

Books and Articles

Bell, Michael. *Food for the Dead*. New York: Basic Books, 2001.

Bicknell, Thomas Williams. *The History of the State of Rhode Island and Providence Plantations, Volume 3*. American Historical Society, 1920.

Brown, Seth. *Rhode Island Curiosities*. Guilford, CT: Globe Pequot Press, 2007.

Buhle, Paul, Scott Molloy, and Gail Sansbury, eds. *A History of Rhode Island Working People*. Providence: Regine Printing Co., 1983.

Chiei, Chris, and Julie Decker, eds. *Quonset Hut: Metal Living for a Modern Age*. New York: Princeton Architectural Press, 2005.

Conley, Patrick T. *Rhode Island's Founders: From Settlement to Statehood*. Charleston, SC: History Press, 2010.

Hawke, D. F. *Nuts and Bolts of the Past*, chapter 9. New York: Harper & Row, Publishers, 1988.

Journal of the Society of Architectural Historians, 1953.

Krasner, Steve. *The Longest Game*. Rhode Island: Gorilla Productions, 1996.

Larson, Timothy W., Esq. "*West v. Barnes:* The First Supreme Court Decision," *Rhode Island Bar Journal* 59, no. 1, July/August 2010.

Mierka,Gregg A. *Rhode Island's Own* (a collection of first-hand accounts of the Civil War; http://suvcw.org/mollus/war/warpapers.htm).

Mills, Barbara. *Providence 1630–1800: Women Are Part of Its History*. Berwyn Heights, MD: Heritage Books, 2002.

Rocky Point Park (RI), Images of America. Charleston, SC: Arcadia Publishing, 2009.

Shelton, Robert. *No Direction Home: The Life and Music of Bob Dylan*. New York: Da Capo Press, 1986, pp. 301–304.

Sifakis, Stewart. *Who Was Who in the Civil War*. New York: Facts on File Publishing, 1988.

White, George Savage. *Memoir of Samuel Slater: The Father of American Manufactures*. Philadelphia: Levi Woodbury, 1836.

Newspapers

Boston Globe

Chicago Tribune

New York Times

Providence Journal

Websites

baseball-reference.com

buffaloreport.com

chepachetfreewill.org

CivilWar.org

constitution.org

cottontimes.co.uk

encyclopedia-titanica.org

Gaspee.org

gendisasters.com

GoLocalProv.com

guinnessworldrecords.com

History.com

jamestown-ri.info

libcom.org

minorleaguebaseball.com

nelights.com

philipmarshall.net

projectundercover.org

quahog.org

RIroads.com

rogerwilliams.org

Tennisfame.com

TennisTheme.com

thekennedyway.com

thewampanoag.com

whipple.org

Wikipedia.org

INDEX

A

Almy, William, 52
Anglican Church, 2
Antinomians, 4, 14
Arkwright, Sir Richard, 50

B

Barnes, David, 47
baseball, 81
baseball's longest game, 102
blizzard, 99
Bradford, William Jr., 47
Brown, Mercy, 74
Brown, Moses, 29, 51
Brown, Obadiah, 53
Brown, Smith, 52
Burnside, Ambrose Everett, 65
Burnside carbine, 68
Butler, Brian, 114

C

Church of England, 10
Civil War, 69
Cocumscussoc, 2
Columbus, 39
company towns, 55
corruption, 109
Country Party, 43, 47

D

Derderian, Jeffrey, 114
Derderian, Michael, 114
Diana, 38
DiPrete, Edward, 109
Dorr, Thomas Wilson, 60
Dyer, Mary (Barrett), 13
Dylan, Bob, 94

F

Floyd, John B., 68
forcing act, the, 44
Franklin, Benjamin, 51

G

Gamecock, 38
Gaspee, 24, 38
Glyn, William E., 73
Great White, 113

H

Hall carbine, 68
Hannah, 25
Harry P. Knowlton, 77
Hatch, Richard, 118
Hopkins, Esek, 37

I
Independence Day, 33
Industrial Revolution, 50

K
Kennedy, Jacqueline Bouvier, 88
Kennedy, John Fitzgerald, 88
King Philip's War, 17
King, Samuel Ward, 60

L
Larchmont, 77
Luther, Seth, 61

M
Massasoit, 17
Metacom, 17
Metacomet, 17

N
National Rifle Association, 70
national tennis championship, first, 72
New England Confederation, 20
Newport Folk Festival, 94
nightclub fire, 113

O
Olney, James, 57

P
paper money, 41
Pennsylvania Society for the Encouragement of Manufactures and Useful Arts, 51
People's Constitution, 62

pirates, 37
Providence, 37
Providence Arcade, 56

Q
Quakers, 14
Quonset huts, 84

R
Revolutionary War, 24, 37
"Rhode Island System," 55
river relocation, 106
"Rogues' Island," 41
Rose, 38
Russillo, Mario, 91
Russo, Ralph, 91
Ruth, Babe, 81

S
scrip, 43
Sears, Richard D., 73
separatism, 9
sideburns, 65
Slater Mill, 54
Slater, Samuel, 50
Slatersville, 55
slavery, 29
sock, world's largest, 121
spinning frame, 50
Station, The, 113
Strutt, Jedediah, 50
Survivor, 118

T
tea party, 35
tuberculosis, 74

U

US Supreme Court decision, first, 46
US Tennis Association, 72

V

vampire, 74
Verin, Jane, 4

W

Warren, Russell, 58
water frame, 50
West v. Barnes, 48
West, William, 46
Whipple, Abraham, 37
Williams, Roger, 1, 4, 8, 19, 34, 41

ABOUT THE AUTHOR

Former *Providence Journal* columnist Seth Brown writes his award-winning weekly column, "The Pun Also Rises," for the *North Adams Transcript,* and occasional reviews for the *Berkshire Eagle* and *USA Today.* He has written four books, including *Rhode Island Curiosities* and *From God to Verse.* His website is www.RisingPun.com.